THE BEST
SOUTHERN
FRONT RANGE
HIKES

D1602910

Huerfano Trailhead.

THE COLORADO
MOUNTAIN CLUB
GUIDEBOOK

THE BEST
SOUTHERN
FRONT RANGE
HIKES

GREG LONG

The Colorado Mountain Club Press
Golden, Colorado

The Best Southern Front Range Hikes

PUBLISHED BY

The Colorado Mountain Club Press
710 10th Street, Suite 200, Golden, Colorado 80401
303-996-2743 I e-mail: cmcpress@cmc.org

Founded in 1912, The Colorado Mountain Club is the largest outdoor recreation, education, and conservation organization in the Rocky Mountains. Look for our books at your local bookstore or outdoor retailer or at www.cmc.org/books.

CONTACTING THE PUBLISHER

We would appreciate it if readers would alert us to any errors or outdated information by contacting us at the address above.

Erika Arroyo: design, composition, and production
Joyce Dunne: copyeditor
Christian Green: publisher

Cover Photo: West Peak Trail, near Cordova Pass, with West Spanish Peak in background, by Todd Caudle.

DISTRIBUTED TO THE BOOK TRADE BY
Mountaineers Books
1001 SW Klickitat Way, Suite 201, Seattle, WA 98134, 800-553-4453
www.mountaineersbooks.org

TOPOGRAPHIC MAPS are copyright 2010 and were created using National Geographic TOPO! Outdoor Recreation software (www.natgeomaps.com), 800-962-1643

We gratefully acknowledge the financial support of the people of Colorado through the Scientific and Cultural Facilities District of greater metropolitan Denver for our publishing activities.

First Edition

ISBN 978-1-937052-01-0

Printed in Korea

To my siblings,
a boisterous band of genuine good,
my life is better—and far less boring—because of you.

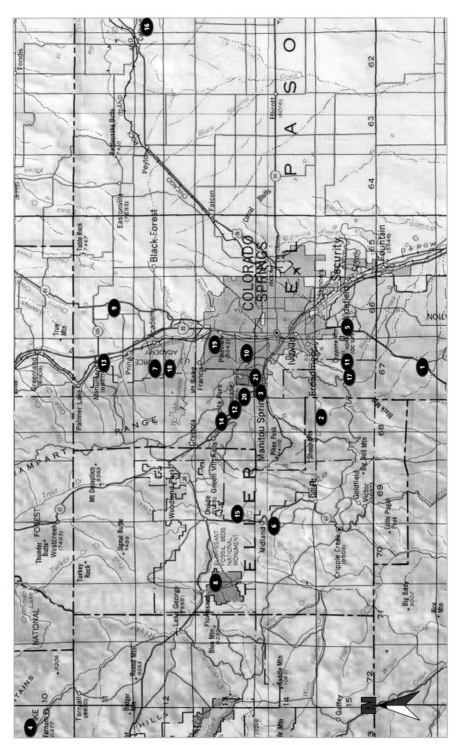

COLORADO SPRINGS AND VICINITY

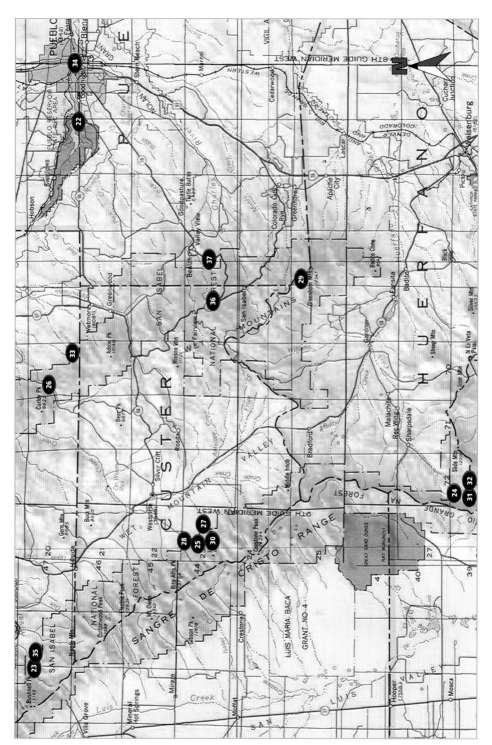

PUEBLO AND VICINITY

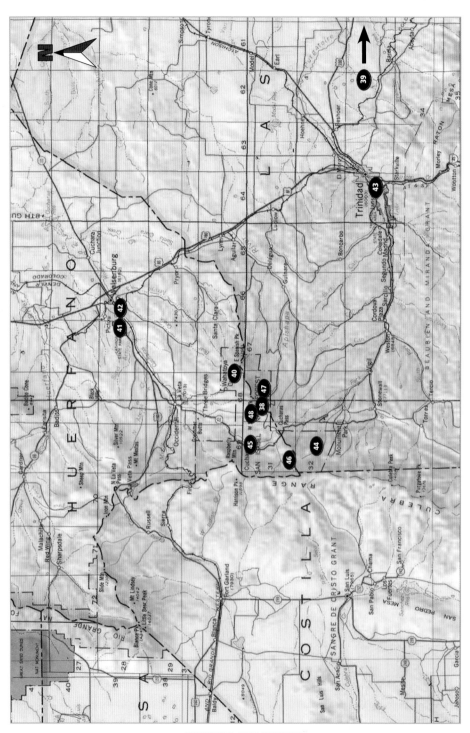

TRINIDAD AND VICINITY

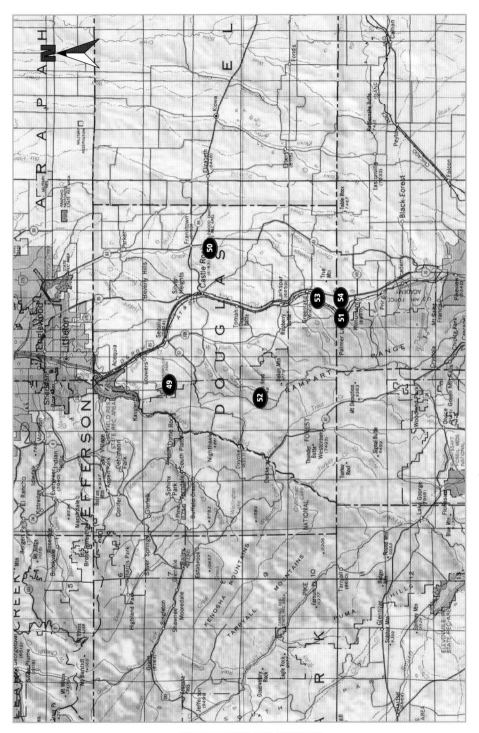

CASTLE ROCK AND VICINITY

Contents

WITHIN 60 MILES OF TRINIDAD

WITHIN 60 MILES OF CASTLE ROCK

Acknowledgments

I'd like to thank the members of The Colorado Mountain Club (CMC) for their continued support of the pack guide series. Many members stepped forward to suggest favorite hikes or point me to new areas I hadn't yet explored. Ultimately, this book is the collaborative effort of several CMC members: Bill Brown, Bill Houghton, Brittany Nielson, Carol Nugent, Dan Anderson, Eric Hunter, and Eric Swab. I could not have done it without their guidance and suggestions in choosing hikes or their efforts in scouting, mapping, and writing up the trails. It is a privilege to work with such fantastic volunteers.

Additional thanks go to Doug Hatfield, Tony Eichstadt, Kristina Kilcoyne, Paul Doyle, Uwe Sartori, Sharon Adams, and Dwight Sunwall.

Fresh snow on the trail to Curley Peak.   PHOTO BY GREG LONG

Introduction

Welcome to *The Best Southern Front Range Hikes*! This book includes more than 50 of the best hikes in the southern Front Range. Looking for a short jaunt after work? It's in here. Want a great trip with the family? It's in here. Trying to push your physical and mental limits with a full-day outing? It's in here. Maybe you'd like a secluded spot for quiet meditation? A place to meet and greet fellow hikers? They're in here, too.

We'd like you to consider some facts before you use this book. The foothills of the Front Range start at 6,000 feet above sea level, and six points along the Front Range are higher than 14,000 feet. Prior to going on a hike, please consider these four points:

- Weather and trail conditions can change in a hurry. Don't get caught without basic gear. See the Ten Essentials System on the following page.
- If you aren't acclimated to higher altitudes, some fairly strange things can happen to you physiologically. Never overestimate your abilities.
- Search and rescue volunteers, U.S. park rangers, and local and state police are very good at their jobs; however, it can take them awhile to reach sick or injured hikers, and it can be hazardous and expensive work.
- The trails we hike are a trust passed down to us by prior generations. In turn, we will pass this trust to our children and so forth.

Where is the southern Front Range exactly? We started with the major cities on the Interstate 25 corridor that are south of Denver: Castle Rock, Colorado Springs, Pueblo, and Trinidad. We looked at the many trails located in and near those cities, then branched out to include hikes within an hour's drive of the interstate. While scouting, an hour seemed to be too limiting a measure; some fantastic trails have trailheads that involve driving on dirt or four-wheel-drive roads—those simply take time to drive. We landed, then, on a boundary of approximately 60 miles from the interstate; this perimeter allowed us to include hikes from the eastern Sangre de Cristo Range in addition to the many close-to-town options. It also allowed us to bring the city of Westcliffe into play as a base of operations. From north to south, the book includes hikes in the Rampart Range, the Pikes Peak Massif, the Lost Creek Wilderness, the Wet Mountains, and the Sangre de Cristos. All hikes can be completed in a day from at least one of the major cities listed.

Once the boundaries were drawn, the debates began. A group of veteran hikers gathered to make suggestions and lobby for their favorites to be included.

Pikes Peak from Waldo Canyon.   PHOTO BY GREG LONG

We sought a diversity of hikes, representing all geographic areas and ability levels. The trails in this guide travel within four wilderness areas, five state parks, and numerous city and county parks and open spaces.

How do you decide where to start? Check the "comments" section at the beginning of each trail for information about the terrain and features you'll see. Check the trail statistics for mileage and elevation gain. The trails are rated on a scale from easy to difficult and for the approximate time it takes to hike the trail round trip. Note that these are approximate ratings; one person's easy may be someone else's epic day. Your conditioning, experience at altitude, and that two-year-old you brought along may impact your time. Many of the hikes close to metropolitan areas can be crowded, especially on weekends, but get out of town just a little bit, and you may have a trail to yourself. On more than one occasion—even a holiday weekend—this writer found himself the only one enjoying lunch on a secluded summit or by a backcountry lake. Before heading to one of the more secluded hikes, be sure to have your skills and your gear in order.

If you like this sampling of hikes, consider joining The Colorado Mountain Club. The CMC sponsors numerous outings throughout the state during every weekend of the year. Beyond activities like hiking and climbing, the CMC is a positive force for conservation, preservation, and education throughout the state of Colorado; it also provides a wide array of classes so members can develop their outdoors skills for the safe enjoyment of wild places like those described in this guide. See www.cmc.org for more information.

THE TEN ESSENTIALS SYSTEM

Hiking offers us an inexpensive and healthy way to enjoy our precious natural heritage. There can be risks that go with an outdoor adventure, however, such as encountering bad weather, suffering an injury, or getting lost. Simple advance preparation can greatly increase the likelihood of a safe and comfortable adventure. If you are not already familiar with the Ten Essentials System, take a few minutes to study the following information and, most importantly, incorporate the system into all of your hiking activities.

1. **Hydration.** Water needs vary greatly, but in general carry at least two liters of water. For longer hikes, take along a water purification system. If you don't drink until you are thirsty, you have waited too long. Extra water in your vehicle will allow you to hydrate both before and after your hike.
2. **Nutrition.** Eat a good breakfast before your hike; pack a healthy lunch—fruits, vegetables, carbs, etc.—and carry some extra trail mix and/or a couple of nutrition bars in case of an emergency.
3. **Sun protection.** Include sunglasses, a large-brimmed hat, lip balm, and sunscreen with an SPF rating of 25 or higher.
4. **Insulation (extra clothing).** Colorado weather can change in an instant, at any time of year, so be prepared. Wear wool or synthetic layers of clothing. Cotton clothing retains moisture and does not insulate when it is damp—including from perspiration—so it should not be part of your hiking gear. At all times, carry a rain/wind parka and pants and extra layers of outer clothing. Gloves or mittens, a warm hat, and extra socks can be invaluable, even on a summer hike.
5. **Navigation.** Carry a map of your hiking area and a reliable—not cheap—compass. A GPS unit can add to your ability to navigate; however, it is not a substitute for the map and compass and the ability to use them.
6. **Illumination.** Even if you plan to be back before dark, carry a headlamp or flashlight and extra batteries. A headlamp is probably the better choice—you can keep both hands free while you work or hike. (Hiking in darkness is not recommended if it can be avoided.)
7. **First-aid supplies.** Include a first-aid kit and know how to use it. The kit should include, at a minimum, bandages and gauze, blister protection

such as moleskin, scissors, disinfectant for cuts, toilet paper, and a Ziploc bag for used t.p.

8. **Fire.** Carry waterproof matches, a lighter, fire ribbon or another commercial fire starter. Be sure that all of these items will work in wet, cold, and windy conditions. Cotton dryer lint, steel wool, hardened tree sap, and dry pine needles can serve as kindling. If you are going above timberline, a small stove is a good emergency item to have with you.

9. **Repair kit and tools.** A pocketknife or multipurpose tool, an emergency whistle, a signal mirror, and low-temperature electrician's tape or duct tape are handy for all types of repairs.

10. **Emergency shelter.** Carry a space blanket and parachute or other nylon cord or a bivouac sack. Large plastic leaf-collection bags are handy for use as emergency rain gear, pack covers, and survival shelter.

Aiken Canyon formation.   PHOTO BY BRITTANY NIELSON

View from Eagle Peak Summit.

OTHER OPTIONS Depending on the length of the trip and the season, you may also want to include the following:

- A foam pad for sitting or sleeping on.
- A metal cup to melt snow in. Eating snow as a water source is not recommended.
- A snow shovel. (A plastic disc or metal dish can serve as an emergency substitute.)
- A walking stick. The better ones are spring-loaded and have canted handles. Walking sticks can take a great deal of weight off of your knees and legs while hiking and provide some upper-body workout. Practice planting the tips quietly to avoid annoying your hiking companions and putting forest creatures to flight.

This information is intended as a starting place in your preparations for hiking in Colorado; it does not tell you everything that you need to know in the woods or how to deal with all emergencies. Many programs and publications are available that can increase your knowledge base. Please visit The Colorado Mountain Club's website at www.cmc.org for more information.

1. Aiken Canyon

BY BRITTANY NIELSON

MAP	Trails Illustrated, Pikes Peak/Cañon City, Number 137
ELEVATION GAIN	1,000 feet
RATING	Easy–moderate
ROUND-TRIP DISTANCE	5.4 miles
ROUND-TRIP TIME	2–3 hours
NEAREST LANDMARK	Fort Carson

COMMENT: Aiken Canyon Nature Preserve is in the foothills of the Front Range west of Fort Carson. Known to bird watchers, Aiken Canyon boasts more than 100 species of birds. This 1,600-acre preserve was initially destined to be a gravel pit. The Nature Conservancy intervened to rescue the land, leaving it in almost pristine condition, with no roads, no major construction, and no known history of overgrazing.

The preserve is named after Charles Aiken, an ornithologist who is credited for most of the early knowledge of birds. Aiken studied birds primarily by shooting and collecting them. During his life he collected more than 5,000 skins, which Colorado College later purchased. He was known as a skilled naturalist who had the ability to distinctly hear notes in bird class and mimic those same birdcalls. Aiken lived at a ranch owned by his father on the current site and later moved to Colorado Springs. Aiken also owned a taxidermy business.

Aiken Canyon is more of a preserve than a park, so it is only open Saturdays, Sundays, and Mondays. Dogs, horses, and bikes are not allowed on these trails. Please respect these rules so we can continue to enjoy this great preserve.

This trail looks like a lollipop with two sticks. Start out on an out-and-back trail to the loop. On the opposite side of the loop is another out-and-back trail leading to an old homestead. This leg of the trail can be skipped to shorten the mileage of the overall hike.

GETTING THERE: Take Interstate 25 to exit 140, Nevada/Tejon. Take the second right off the freeway onto Nevada Avenue. Drive south on Nevada for 15 miles, passing Cheyenne Mountain State Park and two Fort Carson gates. Look for the sign for Turkey Creek Recreation Area. At the left turn for Turkey Creek, turn right for Aiken Canyon. Proceed into the trailhead parking lot on the right.

Red Rock formations along the trail.   PHOTO BY BRITTANY NIELSON

THE ROUTE: Pick up the trail behind the information signs near the field station. Follow the trail out to the start of the loop, approximately 0.7 miles beyond the parking lot. The loop trail brings you closer to the foothills. As you approach the foothills, the number of trees increases while striking red rock formations and cliffs peek through them. The trail gradually climbs to a ridge affording spectacular views in all directions. Enjoy the mix of vegetation and red rocks.

A mile beyond the start of the loop is another junction. This junction leaves the loop and proceeds deeper in to the canyon to the ruins of an old homestead. Turn left here to explore the ruins, which are just less than a mile from the loop trail. The homestead belonged to Ira Waterman; further research has revealed that no neighbors remembered anybody living there. The house was standing when the Nature Conservancy acquired Aiken Canyon, but it was seen as a hazard, and the organization knocked it down. It is obvious several structures and an extensive water system once existed here. A small plot of crops is still apparent.

Return to the loop trail, turning left to complete the loop. Enjoy the walk through the tall pines and observe the vegetation as it changes with a gradual drop in elevation. One mile after returning to the loop trail, complete the loop and continue straight on familiar ground toward the trailhead. From here, return 0.7 miles back to the parking lot.

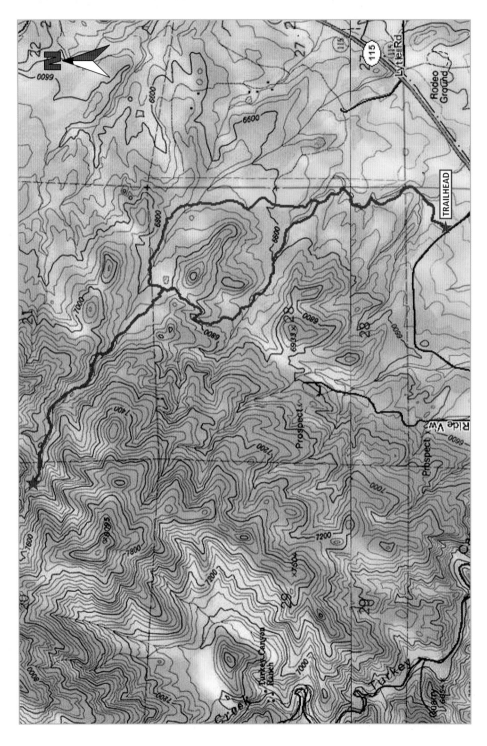

AIKEN CANYON

2. Almagre Mountain

BY GREG LONG

MAP	Trails Illustrated, Pikes Peak/Cañon City, Number 137
ELEVATION GAIN	525 feet for standard route, an additional 500 feet with climb to radio tower and traverse
RATING	Easy–moderate
ROUND-TRIP DISTANCE	3 miles for standard route; 4.25 miles with climb to radio tower and traverse
ROUND-TRIP TIME	1–3 hours
NEAREST LANDMARK	The Broadmoor Hotel

COMMENT: Almagre is the second highest peak in the Colorado Springs area, but nowhere near as well known or as frequently climbed as Pikes Peak. A hike up Almagre may offer a bit of solitude and a unique perspective on its larger and more famous neighbor. Almagre also proves the adage that, sometimes, half the fun is getting there. The hike up Almagre starts with a rough drive up a series of dirt and four-wheel-drive roads that provide as much—if not more—adventure than the hike itself.

You will gain 5,000 feet of elevation on the drive to the trailhead; gaining that much elevation in a short period can challenge the body's ability to adapt to altitude. Be cautious.

GETTING THERE: From Interstate 25, take exit 140, Nevada /Tejon. The second light off the exit ramp is Nevada Avenue. Follow the signs for Colorado 115 South and take exit 46, Lake Avenue. At the Broadmoor Hotel, bear right onto Lake Circle. Head left via the roundabout onto Mesa Drive. Mesa becomes Park then becomes El Pomar. Follow the signs toward the Cheyenne Mountain Zoo. After 0.5 miles, turn right onto Old Stage Road. Check your odometer. Old Stage turns to dirt at 0.8 miles. Pass the Broadmoor stables at 5.6 miles, the St. Peters Dome trail at 7.6 miles, and the Rosemount reservoir at 10.9 miles. Avoid the turn at 11.3 miles and turn right onto Forest Service Road 379 at 12.1 miles. The road becomes rough at this point and a four-wheel-drive vehicle is required. At 16.4 miles, take a sharp right onto Forest Service Road 379A. Continue another 1.6 miles to a gate; park.

A view of the forest below.

THE ROUTE: Climb around the gate and hike along the road for just over a tenth of a mile to the first switchback and the ruins of an old water tank. Turn right and drop down to the ruined dam. This area was formerly the Stratton Reservoir. Follow the dirt track 1.3 miles to the summit. Enjoy views of Pikes Peak from this unusual angle. Binoculars make the summit house and cog railway visible. To the east, check out the runways of the Colorado Springs Airport and Peterson Air Force Base. Return by the same route.

For an additional workout and some off-trail scrambling, try this alternative: Stay on the road at the first switchback and continue up to the radio tower at 1.2 miles. From this sub-peak, enjoy views down to the McReynolds Reservoir. Leave the trail and work your way along the ridge to the north over gentle ups and downs for about a mile before joining the road out to the true summit. Return via the standard route.

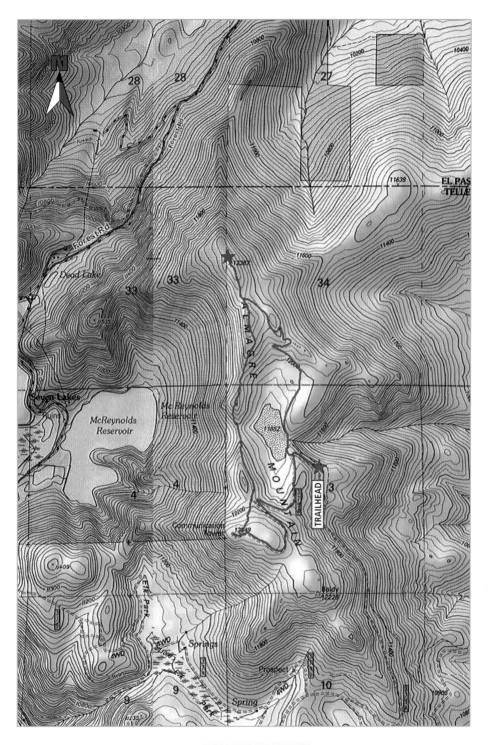

ALMAGRE MOUNTAIN

3. Barr Trail to Pikes Peak
(14,115 feet)

BY KEVIN BAKER

MAP	Trails Illustrated, Pikes Peak/Cañon City, Number 137
ELEVATION GAIN	7,400 feet
RATING	Difficult
ROUND-TRIP DISTANCE	25.8 miles
ROUND-TRIP TIME	9–14 hours
NEAREST LANDMARK	Manitou Springs

COMMENT: Pikes Peak marks the end of the prairie and the beginning of Colorado's vast Rocky Mountains. It was first climbed in 1820 and has since seen millions of visitors, most by way of either the Cog Railway or Pikes Peak Highway. Ironically, Zebulon Pike, for whom the peak is named, never made it to the summit. Katherine Lee Bates was inspired to write "America the Beautiful" atop the mountain, earning Pikes the nickname "America's Mountain." Although not at all technically challenging, a trek up Barr Trail to the summit of Pikes is a worthy accomplishment.

Pikes via Barr Trail has the most vertical gain of any Fourteener in Colorado. A day hike of Pikes is a huge day, so most folks split up the hike into at least two days, with a stay at Barr Camp, some 6.5 miles up the trail, at 10,200 feet. Barr Camp offers many accommodations, including a main bunkhouse, a private cabin, lean-to shelters, and tent sites. Breakfast and dinner are available by reservation, and hot and cold drinks are sold all day. This historic place sees more than 20,000 visitors per year, with most coming in the summer. Visit www. barrcamp.com for information on rates or to make reservations.

GETTING THERE: From US 24, take the Manitou Springs exit and turn west onto Manitou Avenue. Continue 1.4 miles west to Ruxton Avenue. Turn left on Ruxton and continue up this narrow road 1.0 miles to Hydro Street, just beyond the parking area for the Cog Railway. Go right on Hydro and up the steep, narrow street to the trailhead. There is a designated parking lot at the trailhead, which has restrooms. You may leave your car overnight; the fee to park at the trailhead is $5 for 24 hours. Park in any open parking space, and pay at the blue

Trail near Lightning Point.   PHOTO BY PAUL DOYLE

kiosk located at the base of Barr Trail. The kiosk only accepts credit cards. Display the payment receipt in your vehicle window. The kiosk will accept payment for multiple days for overnight trips. On weekends, you may have to park below the cog railway on Ruxton.

THE ROUTE: Barr Trail has a variety of terrain that will challenge every peak-bagger. The first 3.0 miles of trail will test you with a series of switchbacks up the steep southeast slopes. After passing under a natural rock arch, the trail zigs its way steeply up the south slopes, then gradually heads west, contouring along the south slopes of Rocky Mountain.

Continue west at the trail junction with a spur trail that leads to the top of the incline.

After 3.2 miles, a sign at No Name Creek advises Barr Camp is only 3.5 miles away. Most of the vertical to Barr Camp has been completed, and the rest of the way is much easier. Be aware that every trail sign indicating mileage will be incorrect. Head left at the sign, following the creek for a bit. Be sure to stay right at the junction with the unsigned Pipeline Trail. Miss it, and you can end up in Ruxton Park.

After a few more steep switchbacks, the terrain mellows out, and there are flat sections to recuperate on. Some of the best views of Pikes can be obtained by scrambling just off the trail. Lightning Point is a rock outcropping just a few yards off the trail to the south, beyond the *7.8 miles to summit* sign. Monte's View Rockpile is a fun scramble just 1.0 miles from Barr Camp south of the trail, although you'll have to do some rough bushwhacking to get up it.

The section from No Name Creek offers some nice downhill options for a change of pace. After a few steeper sections, you finally arrive at Barr Camp.

Traversing the Face.   PHOTO BY PAUL DOYLE

Barr is a good place to refuel and fill up your water if you're day hiking, although the water is untreated and requires purification. Barr Camp sells Gatorade, bottled water, and snacks.

The second half of the hike to the summit is much tougher, due to the thinning air, but the many switchbacks keep the overall steepness of the trail manageable. I like to break this journey into segments: The first is Barr Camp to the Bottomless Pit Trail. A series of long switchbacks leads up the forest, with beautiful bristlecone pine trees along the way. The trail is quite a bit rockier above Barr Camp, but it is wide and easy to follow. After 1.0 miles, there is a sign for the Bottomless Pit, an enchanting place below the north face of Pikes that few people get a chance to visit. Bottomless Pit is at the base of the Y and Railroad couloirs, a couple of fun, moderate snow climbs for experienced mountaineers using technical climbing gear. Be sure to take the switchback left at this trail junction.

The trail then zigs and zags its way up to A-Frame, a shelter where some opt to camp, near treeline at 12,000 feet. I find this section of the hike to be the longest. In winter, with decent snow conditions, a viable option from treeline is to follow a prominent low-angle gully of snow all the way up to the summit. Other times, follow short switchbacks to around 12,800 feet, at the base of where the east ridge steepens. The trail then does a long traverse across the broad east face, gently climbing 400 feet to a view down into a dramatic bowl known as the Cirque. Enjoy what is probably the most dramatic spot along the trail.

After a few short switchbacks along the edge of the Cirque, there is a sign announcing one mile to the summit. The trail zigs its way up the upper east face, with a few shorter traverses, until the infamous *16 Golden Stairs* sign, a reference to the number of switchbacks left on the trail—there are actually 32. The trail now gets rockier and requires clambering over boulders, but keep pressing on and you'll soon pop out at the end of the train tracks. The summit is not your typical Fourteener, as you will likely be sharing it with tourists who have either ridden the Cog Railway or driven up Pikes Peak Highway.

It is sometimes possible to either ride the train or hitch a ride down, but don't count on it happening. Be prepared to make the long slog all the way back to the bottom. Make certain to visit the true summit of Pikes, amid an indistinct jumble of boulders in the middle of the parking lot. Donuts and pizza are available at the summit house, a rare treat on a Fourteener. Barr Trail is a classic that anyone in decent shape can experience—give it a shot.

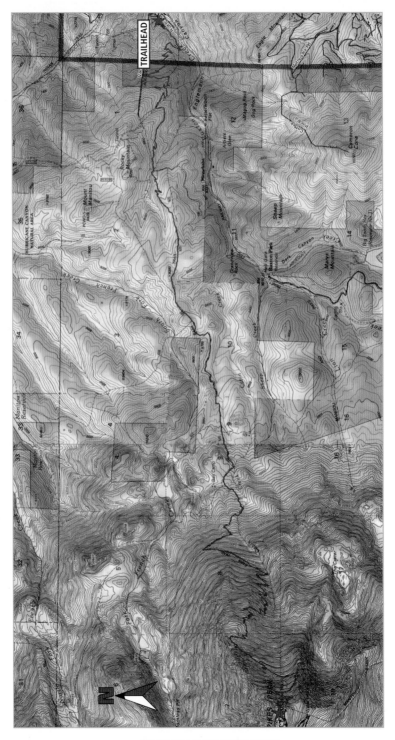

BARR TRAIL TO PIKES PEAK

4. Bison Peak (12,431 feet)

BY GREG LONG

MAP	Trails Illustrated, Tarryall Mountains/Kenosha Pass
ELEVATION GAIN	3,750 feet
RATING	Moderate–difficult
ROUND-TRIP DISTANCE	11.5 miles
ROUND-TRIP TIME	6–8 hours
NEAREST LANDMARK	Tarryall Reservoir

COMMENT: The Lost Creek Wilderness can provide an isolated wilderness experience within an hour's drive of either Denver or Colorado Springs. Despite its proximity to the cities, many of the peaks in the Lost Creek Wilderness see little foot traffic. It may be necessary for two groups to share this marvelous summit on a weekend, but weekdays you can have Bison Peak to yourself. The incredible granite formations throughout the wilderness and especially along the ridge to this summit make a visit to the Lost Creek Wilderness an unforgettable experience.

GETTING THERE: Take US 24 west from Colorado Springs for 37 miles to Lake George, and turn right on Country Road 77. Pass Spruce Grove Campground at 12.8 miles, pass Twin Eagles Campground at 14.4 miles, and reach the Ute Creek trailhead at 19.8 miles.

THE ROUTE: From the parking area, cross the footbridge and hike through meadows and gently uphill for the first 2 miles. The trail then climbs more steeply and steadily through forest to reach the ridgeline and the junction with the Brookside-McCurdy Trail at 4.0 miles. Turn right and follow the Brookside-McCurdy for about a mile as it switchbacks to a high ridge above treeline. Enjoy views of the snowcapped peaks of the Sawatch Range to the west and Pikes Peak to the east. The trail ends abruptly on this ridge. Turn north (left) and traverse for 0.75 miles toward the summit. Be sure to check the landmarks near this turn; should a storm roll in or visibility decrease on the way down, it could be tricky to pick up the trail again.

One of many rock formations near the top of Bison Peak.

At first it may be difficult to determine which pile of rocks is highest. The first obvious large pile isn't the top; the second one is. A survey marker and summit register let you know you're in the right spot. And what a spot it is! Inspect the various convoluted rock formations close at hand or check out the high peaks in the distance. Leave a little extra time and energy, because scrambling up one or two of the rock formations is practically mandatory.

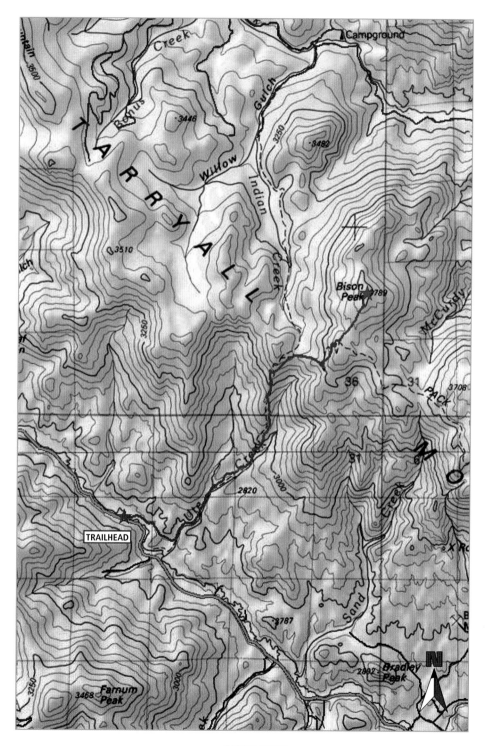

BISON PEAK

5. Cheyenne Mountain State Park Medicine Wheel–Zook Loop, with Blackmer Loop Option

BY BRITTANY NIELSON

MAPS	Trails Illustrated, Pikes Peak/Cañon City, Number 137, Sky Terrain, Colorado Springs and Pikes Peak, or pick one up at the visitor center
ELEVATION GAIN	<200 feet/<500 feet
RATING	Easy–moderate
ROUND-TRIP DISTANCE	1.4 miles/5 miles
ROUND-TRIP TIME	1–3 hours
NEAREST LANDMARK	Fort Carson

COMMENT: Cheyenne Mountain State Park is a 1,680-acre treasure of the Pikes Peak region. The park opened in 2006, and plans are in place for further development. The park hosts 20 miles of developed trails that are great for hiking and biking. Biking in this park ranges from easy to technical. These color-coded trails are well marked, and trail maps are posted at almost every junction.

Cheyenne Mountain, the spectacular backdrop of its park, plays an integral part in US and Canadian military operations. The Cheyenne Mountain Air Force Station sits 2,000 feet inside the mountain. Opened in 1966 as a command station capable of surviving a nuclear attack, the operations inside the mountain remain relevant today. Initially focused on watching foreign air space for possible threats, the station broadened its scope to national air space almost immediately after the second plane plunged into the World Trade Center on September 11, 2001. Today the Cheyenne Mountain Air Force Station tracks every object in the skies in North America, around the world, and into outer space. While enjoying the hike around the park, keep in mind that there are buildings inside that mountain, including a base exchange and even a chapel. (Source: About. com. "Cheyenne Mountain Air Force Station: A Look Inside NORAD": http://usmilitary.about.com/od/jointservices/l/blnorad.htm.)

The park features several developed picnic areas and a campground. The facilities are new, clean, and well maintained. At the time of publication, the entrance fee is $7 per day. Pets are not allowed on trails.

GETTING THERE: Exit Interstate 25 at the Nevada/Tejon, exit 140. Take the second right onto Nevada and continue south for just over 5 miles. Follow the signs for the park and turn right at the traffic light to access Fort Carson Gate 1. Be sure to stop by the visitor center to pick up a map and pay the vehicle fee. The left turn for the trailhead is well marked shortly after passing the entrance station.

Hikers coming from the south should exit Interstate 25 at South Academy Boulevard and turn south onto Colorado 115. Follow the signs into the park by turning right at the traffic light for Fort Carson Gate 1.

THE ROUTE: Proceed on the trail toward the registration station. Register and turn right onto the Zook Loop. Just 0.1 miles beyond the trailhead, take the far left branch of a four-way intersection to remain on the Zook Loop. Taking either trail

Scrub oaks line—and deposit leaves on—the trail.   PHOTO BY BRITTANY NIELSON

A muddy turn in the trail.

to the right leads up to the picnic areas. This section of the Zook Loop is a wide, steady path. After another 0.1 miles, turn right onto the Medicine Wheel Trail.

The Medicine Wheel Trail narrows and begins to climb gently. The trail affords great views of Cheyenne Mountain through pleasant vegetation. It becomes more intimate with the mountain and soon leads to a junction with the tail of the Blackmer loop.

The Blackmer loop leads higher yet up the mountain, although the additional elevation gain is only about 300 feet. The Cheyenne Mountain State Park website (www.parks.state.co.us/park/cheyennemountain/) describes the trail as "[a] park staff favorite because of great pines and rock gardens along the way." An additional 100 feet can be gained by taking the Cougar Trail through thick forest from the top of the Blackmer loop.

Turn right to take the Blackmer loop, making the total trail mileage 5 miles. To do the 1.4-mile loop, turn left and proceed on a slight downhill to the Zook loop. Turn right on the Zook loop.

Once back on the Zook loop, pass a trail on the right about 0.4 miles beyond the trail. Enjoy views of the plains to the east while slowly descending back to the trailhead. Follow the trail straight out to the visible trailhead.

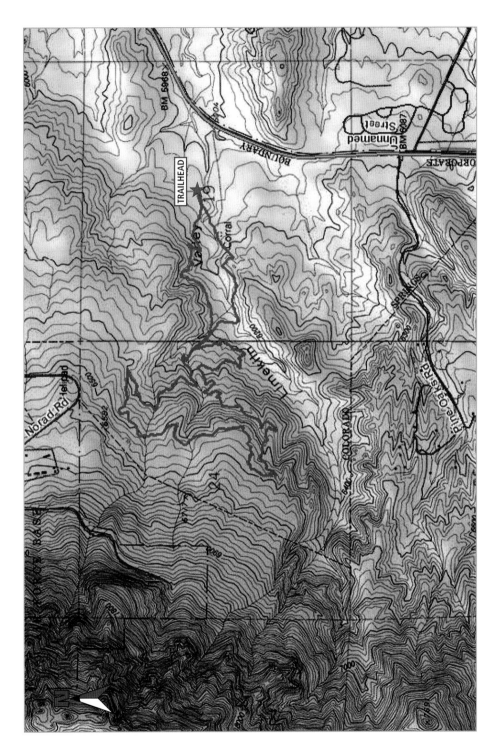

CHEYENNE MOUNTAIN STATE PARK

6. Dome Rock Loop

BY DAN ANDERSON

MAPS	Trails Illustrated, Pikes Peak/Cañon City, Number 137 USGS, Divide; Cripple Creek North, 7.5 minute
ELEVATION GAIN	1,650 feet
RATING	Moderate
ROUND-TRIP DISTANCE	10.5 miles
ROUND-TRIP TIME	5–7 hours
NEAREST LANDMARK	Divide

COMMENT: Would you like to cool off on a hot summer day? Try hiking down the Dome Rock Trail in the Dome Rock State Wildlife Area (SWA) and ford the creek 16 times by staying on the original road and returning the same way. The last half mile of the Dome Rock Trail has views of the massive granite structure called Dome Rock plus other large granite outcrops to the west.

The Willow Creek Trail goes south up a valley to a ridge. It heads west in a roller-coaster fashion along a ridge with superb views of the west side of Pikes Peak and the surrounding area.

Explore more than 25 miles of trails along ridges, in cool valleys, through lovely stands of aspens, and through open meadows. Many trails get little use, and some connect to the trails in Mueller State Park, which borders the northeastern part of Dome Rock SWA.

The western part of the SWA is closed to the public from December 1 through July 15. The Dome Rock Trail west of the Jack Rabbit Lodge ruins (junction of Cabin Creek Trail), Spring Creek Trail, Dome View Trail, and War Party Overlook are closed to the public during that period. Dogs, fires, bicycles, and rock climbing are prohibited at all times.

The Dome Rock Trail, as it follows the original road, crosses Fourmile Creek many times. As of this writing, only the first two crossings have a bridge. Thunderstorms or high water from snow melt early in the season make these creek crossings challenging and even dangerous. There are social trails on the north side that bypass all the crossings, but finding them can be difficult, especially those farthest to the west. Loop hikers using Sand Creek or Spring Creek have to cross Fourmile Creek.

Dome Rock rises above the trail.

PHOTO BY DAN ANDERSON

GETTING THERE: From Colorado Springs take Interstate 25; exit 141 westbound on US 24 (Cimarron Street) toward Manitou Springs. Go 25 miles through Woodland Park to Divide. At the traffic light in Divide turn left (south) on Colorado 67 and go 5.3 miles to Four Mile Road (County Road 61). Veer right on Four Mile Road and go 2.1 miles to the turnoff into the parking areas for Dome Rock SWA.

THE ROUTE: From the southern parking area, go south for 0.1 miles to the Twisted Pine Nature Trail junction, then 1.7 miles on the Willow Creek Trail to the top of a saddle with a four-way junction. If this turn is missed, you will find yourself down the hill at the park boundary. Turn right (west) and continue up the ridge for 0.9 miles to the Sand Creek Trail junction. Continue straight on the Willow Creek Trail for 0.3 miles. The road continues ahead, then left to the boundary. The Spring Creek Trail branches right and downhill. There is a sign here for the winter-spring closure of the Spring Creek Trail.

Go down the Spring Creek Trail for 0.4 miles to the junction of the Dome View Trail, which is 1.8 miles long. The trail could be overgrown with grass. After 0.3 miles, the War Party Overlook Trail branches to the right. Do not expect to see much of a trail, but a water cut of the old road helps to identify it.

Dome Rock Trail.   PHOTO BY DAN ANDERSON

Proceed down the canyon and eventually reach Fourmile Creek; ford it, and, after 2.2 miles, reach the Dome Rock Trail. Continue over a shoulder with great views of Dome Rock and the wide valley, and down the other side. After 1.2 miles through this lovely valley, reach the junction of a social trail that bypasses the next stream crossing, which is just ahead. Continue on the social trail for 0.3 miles to rejoin the old road. After 0.2 miles, find the next social bypass trail junction, go 0.4 miles, and rejoin the old road. The junction of the Cabin Creek Trail is another 0.2 miles ahead. The ruins of the Jack Rabbit Lodge are here, along with a sign about the winter-spring closure boundary.

After the Cabin Creek Trail, it is 0.2 miles to the next social trail junction, then 0.8 miles to rejoin the old road. Continue on the trail for 0.6 miles to another social trail and rejoin the old road after 0.1 miles.

A little farther along the trail, pass the ruins of some cabins and the tailings of an old mine (Sand Burr Mine). Then, after 0.6 miles, cross the creek on a bridge and arrive at the northern parking area.

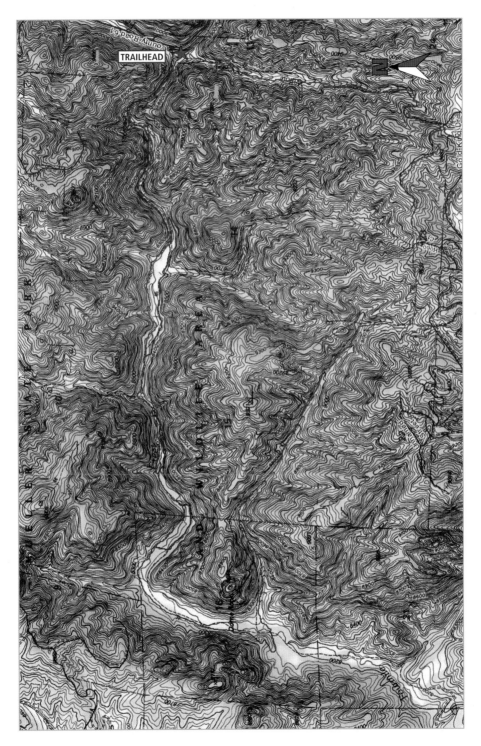

DOME ROCK

7. Eagle Peak

BY BILL BROWN

MAPS	Trails Illustrated, Pikes Peak/Cañon City, Number 137, Pikes Peak Atlas
ELEVATION GAIN	2,100 feet
RATING	Moderate
ROUND-TRIP DISTANCE	4 miles
ROUND-TRIP TIME	3–5 hours
NEAREST LANDMARK	Air Force Academy Visitor Center

COMMENT: The hike begins on the Air Force Academy grounds. As of 2011, most of the academy is closed to anyone who does not have a US Department of Defense identification card. This effectively precludes the general public from using popular trails like Stanley Canyon and the Falcon Trail. The exception is the Eagle Peak/Goat Camp Creek Trail, which is accessed from one of the few locations open to the public: the Air Force Academy Visitor Center.

The hike up Goat Camp Creek is steep and wild. It passes beside a stream with several little waterfalls, flowing fast in the spring runoff and slowing to a trickle by fall. About halfway up, the route crosses Goat Camp Creek and climbs out of the drainage to a pleasant meadow filled with aspens and (in summer) brilliant wildflowers. This meadow is on the west side of Eagle's summit, about a quarter mile and 500 vertical feet above.

The climb is strenuous and the route filled with hazards: boulders, roots, deadfall, and scree. Some big natural steps can be especially challenging. Bikes and horses dare not venture here. Snowshoers will find the route marginal at best.

GETTING THERE: From Interstate 25, take exit 156B (North Gate Boulevard) west. Enter the Air Force Academy's North Gate within a half mile. At the gate, you will be stopped and probably asked to show your driver's license and vehicle registration. Your vehicle may also be searched. Once past the gate, follow signs for the visitor center. Continue west on North Gate Boulevard; it becomes Academy Boulevard, then curves southward. After about 4 miles

Pikes Peak can be seen in the distance.

PHOTO BY TONY EICHSTADT

from the gate, turn into the visitor center. Park on the west end of the upper level of the parking lot.

There are internal security checkpoints within the academy, so be sure to exit the by the same route.

THE ROUTE: Start by walking west about 100 yards to cross Academy Boulevard. Walk north along the west side of the street for 40 yards, then head west up Pavilion Drive, a gravel service road. Eagle Peak's bold summit and sheer rock outcrop on the eastern face is ahead and a couple thousand feet above. Continue past an electrical substation. At mile 0.5, the main road bends right at a *Government Vehicles Only Beyond This Point* sign. Continue straight (west) on the gravel road another 80 yards, where this road turns northward. Here, find a sign describing the challenges and hazards of the route.

From the sign, start up a single track trail through gambel oak, ponderosa pine, and Douglas fir. Soon you will leave Air Force property and enter Pike

Looking down to the Air Force Academy Chapel and grounds.   PHOTO BY TONY EICHSTADT

National Forest. At about mile 0.75 from your start at the parking lot, you enter the main drainage of Goat Camp Creek. You will stay in or along the north side of this drainage for the next half mile, climbing with effort through a variety of natural obstacles. The steep canyon walls provide welcome cooling for a summer hike. Pause to enjoy a small waterfall, then climb over a big tree and associated roots. About 300 yards beyond, be alert for an obscure crossing to the south side of the drainage.

The still-wild trail climbs west then southwest for about 0.3 miles to the relief of a tranquil aspen meadow. This is a good place to refresh and enjoy the ambience before pushing on. From the meadow the trail ascends steeply east-southeast toward the summit. The first part of the route is rocky, braided, and badly eroded. Scramble over some talus for the final few feet to the summit. Here you get your reward of 360-degree views, with especially fine perspectives on the Air Force Academy and Pikes Peak.

Retrace your steps—with caution—for the return to the trailhead.

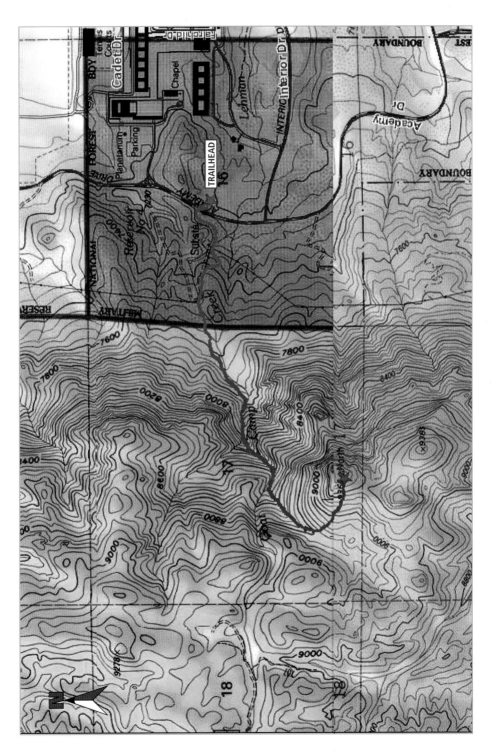

EAGLE PEAK

8. Florissant Fossil Beds National Monument

BY DAN ANDERSON

MAPS	Trails Illustrated, Pikes Peak/Cañon City, Number 137
	USGS, Lake George, 7.5 minutes
ELEVATION GAIN	750 feet
RATING	Easy
ROUND-TRIP DISTANCE	5.2 miles
ROUND-TRIP TIME	2–3.5 hours
NEAREST LANDMARK	Florissant

COMMENT: Did you know there were once redwood trees with a circumference of 41 feet or more in Colorado?

Florissant Fossil Beds National Monument preserves petrified redwood tree stumps and fossils found in the shale of an ancient lake. It also provides the opportunity, through the Hornbek Homestead, to learn some history of the area and how people lived in the late 1800s.

The Ponderosa Loop Trail is 0.4 miles and wheelchair accessible. It passes exhibits and petrified stumps and leads to the amphitheater. The Sawmill Trail branches off of this trail on the northwest and southeast ends.

The 1-mile Petrified Forest Loop goes north from the visitor center through the grassy valley. It passes the Big Stump and other, smaller stumps and provides access to the Scudder quarry. Signs along the trail provide a timeline of the Earth's history.

During the summer, the park is open from 8:00 a.m. to 6:00 p.m. From Labor Day to Memorial Day, the park is open from 9:00 a.m. to 5:00 p.m. except for major winter holidays. The park is only open for day use. The entrance fee is $3.00 per person over 16 years of age. Pets are not allowed on the trails.

As of this writing, the visitor center is being torn down to be replaced by a new one. The new construction will result in some trail changes. The park has about 14 miles of trails to enjoy nature and take in scenic views. Be aware that lightning during thunderstorms can strike anywhere in this park.

GETTING THERE: From Colorado Springs take Interstate 25, then exit 141 westbound on US 24 (Cimarron Street) toward Manitou Springs. Go 33.2 miles

Boulder Creek Trail.   PHOTO BY DAN ANDERSON

through Woodland Park and Divide to Florissant. Turn left (south) on Teller County Road 1 and go 2.4 miles to the turnoff on the right (west) into Florissant Fossil Beds National Monument.

THE ROUTE: As of this writing, the Petrified Forest Loop starts at the parking lot and goes north-northeast for 0.1 miles to the junction of the Hornbek Wildlife Loop. A new trail has been added behind and west of the visitor center and east of the covered stumps. This trail should not be confused with the west side of the Petrified Forest Loop, which is found west of the covered stumps. These directions may change once the new visitor center is built.

Go northeast about 0.17 miles on the new trail to the junction of the Hornbek Wildlife loop. From the Petrified Forest loop, go east 0.9 miles on the Hornbek Wildlife loop to the junction of Twin Rock Trail (sign also mentions Shootin' Star Trail). Turn left (northwest) and go 0.7 miles to the Hornbek Homestead. Look around the site to see how people lived in the 1880s.

Find the continuation of the loop trail on the north side of the homestead heading west, then south. From the homestead, go 1.1 miles to the junction of

Aspens along Boulder Creek Trail.

the Boulder Creek Trail and continue ahead, southwest, for 0.8 miles to a large pile of boulders. Children will enjoy the "caves" in the boulders. Continue 0.8 miles to the Sawmill Trail junction. Turn left, cross a bridge, and go 0.2 miles to the Boulder Creek/Hornbek loop junction. Continue to the right for 0.3 miles to the Ponderosa loop junction. Continue through the exhibit area for 0.14 miles back to the visitor center.

ALTERNATE ROUTE

From the Hornbek Wildlife loop, hike out and back on the Twin Rock Trail (2.2 miles one way) to see additional interesting boulders. Or increase the mileage of the loop about 1 mile by taking, from the Boulder Creek Trail, the Sawmill Trail back to the visitor center. The Sawmill Trail has views of Pikes Peak.

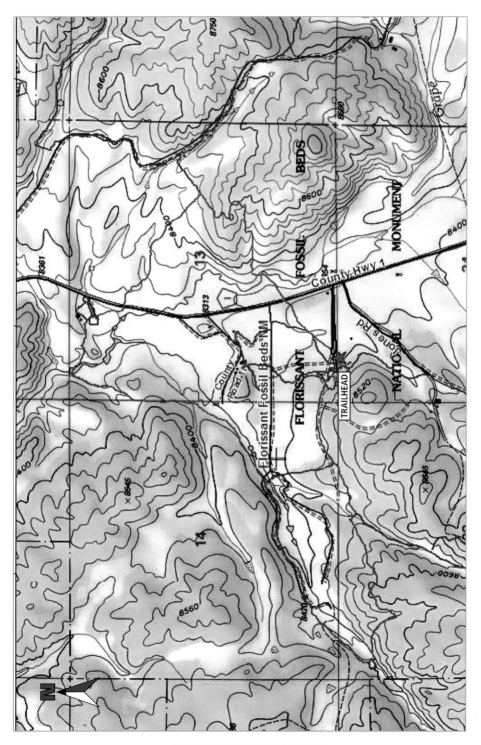

FLORISSANT FOSSIL BEDS TRAIL

9. Fox Run Regional Park— North Loop

BY BRITTANY NIELSON

MAP	Sky Terrain, Colorado Springs and Pikes Peak
ELEVATION GAIN	<200 feet
RATING	Easy
ROUND-TRIP DISTANCE	1.5 miles
ROUND-TRIP TIME	½–1 hour
NEAREST LANDMARK	Interstate 25 and Baptist Road

COMMENT: Fox Run Regional Park lies just 3 miles east of Interstate 25 in Black Forest. In addition to 5 miles of multi-use trails, the park boasts open grass fields, playgrounds, pavilions, and ponds. Fox Run can be accessed at the trailhead listed below or via the main park entrance on Stella Road. This park is a gem of the Black Forest area and a great family retreat. There is no fee to enter the park.

Trails in Fox Run Park are family-friendly, wide, and gentle in elevation gain. The park's elevation ranges from 7,212 feet to 7,528 feet. Interpretive signs along the trail provide information about the surrounding flora as you move through the ponderosa pine forest. Trail junctions are marked clearly, and official junctions include posted maps to make route finding and improvisation easy. These trails are great for kids, bicyclists who do not want anything technical, and cross-country skiers after a good snowstorm.

Be aware that Fox Run Regional Park is home to wildlife activity. Be especially "bear aware" and ensure that children are kept close. Please also be sure to carry all food and trash out.

Watch for horses and bikes on the trail. Bikers and hikers yield to horses. Bikers yield to hikers.

GETTING THERE: Exit Interstate 25 at Baptist Road, exit 158. Head east up the hill 4 miles and turn right (south) on Roller Coaster Road. Look for the Roller Coaster Trailhead on the right in about 0.25 miles. There is a restroom facility at the trailhead.

THE ROUTE: Follow the path past the restroom and then to the right. Turn left at the two signs to cross a small bridge and head uphill. Once on top of the

A sunny day for a hike.   PHOTO BY BRITTANY NIELSON

ridge, Pikes Peak presents short, teasing views through the screen of ponderosa pines. After about 0.25 miles, pass a trail junction on the right and stay straight. Shortly after, pass a spur trail to the right and turn left. At the next junction, pass a trail to the left and head right down toward the parking lot.

This parking lot is the Fallen Timber Trailhead, accessible using the Fox Run entrance on Stella Road. Head past the restroom to the trail directly across the parking lot. Pick up the trail on the obvious wide path marked by two short signs.

Just over 0.1 miles beyond the Fallen Timber Trailhead is a trail to the left. This trail leads to the West Loop trails. The West Loop trails head west and south toward the main area of the park, which features playgrounds and fields. If 1.5 miles is not a long-enough hike, turn here for additional mileage. To continue on the North Loop Trail, do not turn. Instead, go straight past the trail to the West Loop. Just less than 0.2 miles beyond the first junction, arrive at a spur trail that goes under Baptist Road. Turn right here and head uphill.

Once up the hill, enjoy the rolling hills and a small, young aspen stand. This diversity in the ponderosa forest is welcome, as aspens are known for their autumn beauty.

Another 0.2 miles down the trail, encounter the last junction. Head straight toward the restroom and parking area.

FOX RUN REGIONAL PARK—NORTH LOOP

10. Garden of the Gods— Central Garden/ Rockledge Ranch Loop

BY BRITTANY NIELSON

MAPS	Trails Illustrated, Pikes Peak/Cañon City, Number 137, Sky Terrain, Colorado Springs and Pikes Peak, or pick one up at the Garden of the Gods Visitor Center
ELEVATION GAIN	<500 feet
RATING	Easy
ROUND-TRIP DISTANCE	3 miles
ROUND-TRIP TIME	1–2 hours
NEAREST LANDMARK	Garden of the Gods Visitor Center

COMMENT: This is a great route for families. It includes easy trails, a stroll through the dramatic central garden, and a visit to a historic, working ranch with farm animals.

Most of the trails in the Garden are multi-use. The park is open from 5:00 a.m. to 11:00 p.m. May 1 to October 31 and from 5:00 a.m. to 9:00 p.m. November 1 to April 30.

GETTING THERE: Exit Interstate 25 at Garden of the Gods, exit 146, and drive west 2.25 miles. Turn left at 30th Street and enter Garden of the Gods in 1.5 miles via Gateway Road on the right. Follow the road to the right onto Juniper Way Loop. At the first fork, approximately 1.5 miles after entering the park, go left and follow the signs to the visitor center. After passing Ridge Road, look for the South Garden parking area on the right and park. Please note the bike lane on the right side of the road is not for cars; cars pulling into this lane can pose a hazard to bicyclists.

THE ROUTE: Access the Ute Trail at the south end of the parking area. This is the trail closest to the parking entrance. Stay on this trail for about 0.25 miles until arriving at the signed right turn for Niobrara (note, you may see a sign pointing straight to Niobrara before you arrive at the junction). Cross Ridge Road and proceed on the Buckskin Charley Trail. Turn left at the first

Gray Rock at Garden of the Gods.

junction toward another junction. Take a moment to go straight and enjoy the views and photo opportunity. After coming down from the overlook, turn left (north).

The Buckskin Charley Trail instantly gives way to a dazzling view of Pikes Peak. Enjoy views of the massive fins Sleeping Giant, Gray Rock, and Kissing Camels. Pass two trails on the left before turning right onto the Scotsman Trail. Continue on the Scotsman to the road and cross onto a paved sidewalk.

This is the Central Garden and is the most dramatic—and crowded—portion of this hike. Follow the sidewalk from the road to the sign and turn right on the dirt trail marked *Upper Loop*. At the top of the loop is a small area with some rocks to crawl around on. Please note that most of this area is off limits.

Rock formations.

Climbing without a permit, proper training, or equipment is not only dangerous but also against the law.

After completing this loop, turn right onto the paved sidewalk and take three more rights to loop around Gray Rock and head southeast toward the road. Cross Juniper Way to the left and Gateway Road to the right. Proceed on Chambers Trail and take a quick left onto Galloway Homestead Trail. Follow this trail around the other side of the ridge as it wraps to the right. Continue south to the turnoff for Rock Ledge Ranch. Turn left to detour to the ranch, visit the animals, see the crops, and take part in some local history.

This route continues straight on the Galloway Homestead Trail. Pass an unofficial trail on the right and then turn left on the Ute Trail. Take the first right on the Ute Trail Connection (the sign was missing at this junction at the time of publication; look for a clearly marked intersection with a post missing a sign on the trail to the right). Follow the Ute Trail Connection up to the ridge. Once on top of the ridge, take a quick spur trail to an overlook on the right, then head straight down to the parking lot.

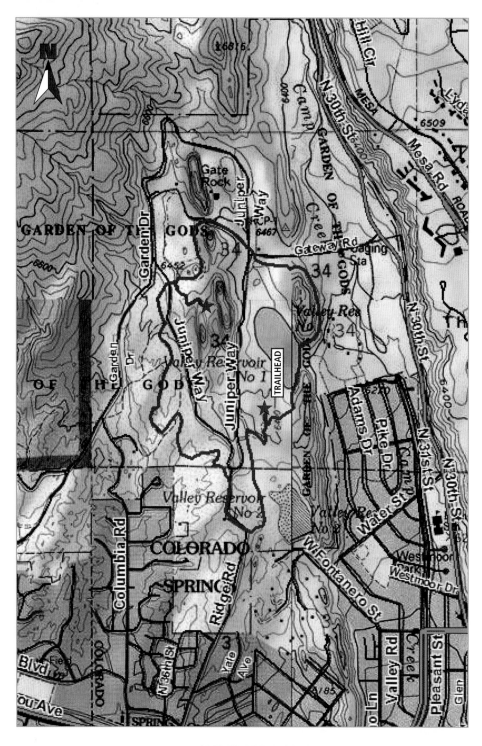

GARDEN OF THE GODS

11. Grayback Peak

BY GREG LONG

MAP	Trails Illustrated, Pikes Peak/Cañon City, Number 137
ELEVATION GAIN	1,100 feet
RATING	Easy–moderate
ROUND-TRIP DISTANCE	3.5 miles
ROUND-TRIP TIME	2–4 hours
NEAREST LANDMARK	The Broadmoor Hotel

COMMENT: Grayback Peak gives great views and a mountain climbing experience without an extreme effort. It is one of many peaks along the Front Range where—at certain times during the fall—ladybugs swarm the tops as an annual ritual. Although wooded, the summit offers views of Pikes Peak as well as south along the Front Range all the way to the Spanish Peaks.

GETTING THERE: From Interstate 25, take exit 140, Nevada /Tejon. The second light off the exit ramp is Nevada. Follow the signs for Colorado 115 south and take exit 46, Lake Avenue. At the Broadmoor Hotel, bear right onto Lake Circle. Take the roundabout to head to the left on Mesa Drive. Mesa becomes Park Street, then becomes El Pomar Street. Follow the signs toward the Cheyenne Mountain Zoo. After 0.5 miles, turn right onto Old Stage Road. Check your odometer. Old Stage turns to dirt at 0.8 miles. Pass the Broadmoor stables at 5.6 miles, and turn left at 6.1 miles onto Forest Road 371 toward Emerald Valley Ranch. Follow this road 0.25 miles to a turnout at the top of a hill on the left. This last quarter mile may be rough for passenger cars, but it should be passable.

THE ROUTE: From the parking area, take the trail uphill to the left. This area sees heavy equestrian use and the trail is eroded in places. After 0.5 miles, reach a minor summit, then descend slightly at 0.75 miles before ascending to a false summit at 1 mile. This small open area has an overlook and is a great place for a break or a possible turnaround spot for those traveling with younger children; check out the views west to rock formations. Continue on the trail 0.5 miles past this overlook and come to a fork marked by a rock cairn. The main trail appears to go left and uphill; instead, bear right (straight) and contour along the ridge. Stay alert; this turn is easily missed. After traversing along the ridge,

Looking toward the top of Grayback Peak.

the trail ascends to the wooded summit. The shoulder of Pikes Peak is visible to the north, and the Spanish Peaks are visible to the south. Be sure to check for ladybugs before grabbing a seat on the summit rocks. Return the way you came.

SIDEBAR: THE LADYBUG PHENOMENON

Watch where you sit! You might crush a ladybug, or two, or 1,000 if you pick the wrong rock. In a pattern that continues to defy precise explanation, one species of ladybug—the Convergent Lady Beetle—congregates in large numbers at the top of certain peaks in the late summer and early fall. Among the theories are that the peaks are good protection from predators and that the mountains are a good spot for mating. Whatever the reason, many mountain summits host ladybugs by the thousands; these summits usually sit between 8,000 and 10,000 feet, but sometimes the phenomenon has been seen higher. Hikes in this guide where the ladybug phenomenon has been observed include Grayback Peak, Devils Head, and East Spanish Peak.

Ladybugs cover a rock on the summit.

GRAYBACK PEAK

12. Heizer Trail

BY GREG LONG

MAP	Trails Illustrated, Pikes Peak/Cañon City, Number 137
ELEVATION GAIN	1,900 feet
RATING	Moderate
ROUND-TRIP DISTANCE	5 miles
ROUND-TRIP TIME	2–3 hours
NEAREST LANDMARK	Green Mountain Falls

COMMENT: The Heizer Trail is a hidden gem near Colorado Springs. Frequented by Cascade and Green Mountain Falls locals, it doesn't see much traffic otherwise. The trail can be a quick out-and-back hike or a gateway into the Pikes Peak trail system and possible extended hikes with car shuttles. Out and

The trailhead for Heizer Trail.

PHOTO BY GREG LONG

Enjoying views along the trail.

back makes for a great morning or afternoon getaway and is the trip described here.

GETTING THERE: From Colorado Springs, take Colorado 24 West for 9 miles to the exit for Pikes Peak Highway. Turn left at the traffic light and almost immediately turn left onto Emporia Street. Parking is available at the park located at the base of Anemone Hill Road. Walk 100 feet up that road to the start of the trail. The trail begins on private property; please be respectful so the owners will continue to allow access.

THE ROUTE: The trail begins with a series of switchbacks for a half mile. Enjoy views down to the tourist wonderland of Santa's Workshop and its Ferris wheel and the cars heading up Pikes Peak. Pause to appreciate being human powered and heading into the wilderness. At 1.5 miles, reach a rock outcropping with views overlooking the state highway as it climbs Ute Pass and of Pikes Peak Highway as it works its way up the peak. Continue on switchbacks to the top of the ridge, leaving the highways behind to enjoy the now flatter trail and views toward the summit of Pikes Peak. Scramble over to the rocks on either side of the trail for a different perspective. At 2.2 miles, reach the highpoint of the trail. Turn here, or continue downhill for 0.4 miles to a sign indicating a watershed area and then turn. A quick scramble up the rocks to the left of the trail provides further views of Pikes Peak and Cameron Cone.

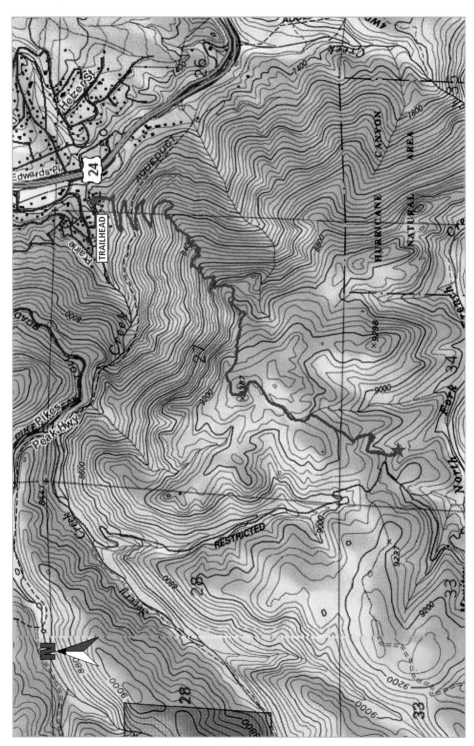

HEIZER TRAIL

13. Monument Rock Loop

BY GREG LONG

MAP	Trails Illustrated, Pikes Peak/Cañon City, Number 137
ELEVATION GAIN	200 feet
RATING	Easy
ROUND-TRIP DISTANCE	2.5 miles
ROUND-TRIP TIME	1–1.5 hours
NEAREST LANDMARK	Monument

COMMENT: The trail system around Monument Rock is well known to locals in the Tri-Lakes area, many of whom make it a daily workout. Strangers to the area will be surprised to find such a variety of trails and terrain just a few minutes from the interstate. The loop presented here is just a small sample of what's available within the trail system. Most routes last from 1 to 3 hours; however, it's possible to connect with forest trails higher up Mt. Herman and make a full day of it. The trail is frequented by hikers, dog walkers, equestrians, and mountain bikers, so be prepared to share.

GETTING THERE: Take Interstate 25 to the Monument exit (exit 161). From the northbound ramp, turn left at the traffic light at the end of the exit ramp onto Colorado 105. Cross over Interstate 25 and go straight through the traffic lights;

First view of Monument Rock on the trail.   PHOTO BY GREG LONG

Mt. Herman looms above the trail.   PHOTO BY GREG LONG

don't follow Colorado 105 (Colorado 105 turns right, and the road you are on becomes Second Street). From the southbound ramp, turn left directly onto Second Street.

Follow Second Street to the stop sign just past the railroad tracks. This is Mitchell Avenue. Turn left and follow Mitchell Avenue for 0.6 miles. Turn right onto Mt. Herman Road and continue 0.75 miles to Nursery Road. Turn left and into the parking lot.

THE ROUTE: The trails in this area include many crisscrossed social trails, and it is easy to get turned around and off route. Remember that all trails leave west (toward the mountains) from the parking lot; therefore, the way home is always east, away from the mountains. Start at the trailhead sign and go straight at the initial intersection, passing through a fence and downhill at 0.3 miles. Reach a dirt road at 0.75 miles and turn left. Hike on the road for about 750 feet; the destination is in sight. Be wary of a closed trail leading right; wait until you reach a stand of pine trees, then turn right on a trail toward the rock. Reach the rock at 1.2 miles; there are some old benches near the rock, and it is possible to do some scrambling on the large formation. To complete the loop, turn right at the rock for 200 yards, then a hard right back toward the trailhead. Reach the road again at 1.75 miles. Turn left, go through the gate, and in 100 feet, turn right onto the trail. Take a last left fork at 2.5 miles to return to the trailhead.

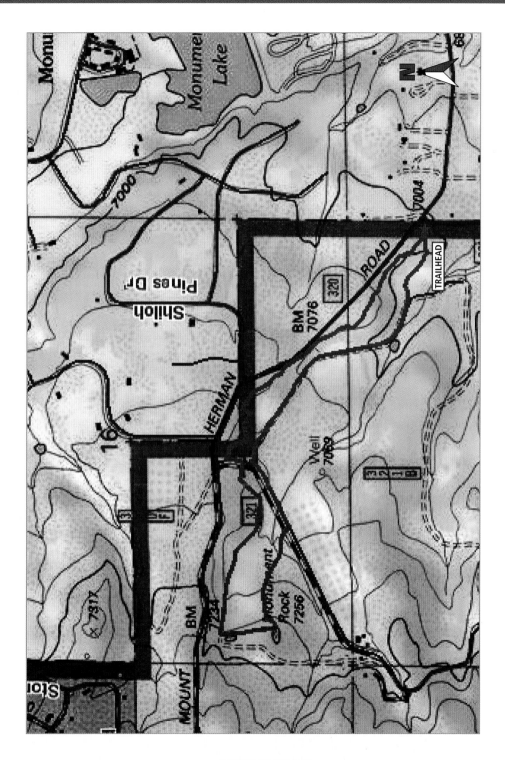

MONUMENT ROCK

14. Mount Esther

BY GREG LONG

MAP	Trails Illustrated, Pikes Peak/Cañon City, Number 137
ELEVATION GAIN	1,500 feet
RATING	Moderate
ROUND-TRIP DISTANCE	Standard route = 5 miles From Crow Gulch = 4.7 miles
ROUND-TRIP TIME	3–5 hours
NEAREST LANDMARK	Green Mountain Falls

COMMENT: Mount Esther has twin summits; although they are wooded, rock formations and openings provide excellent views of Pikes Peak and the surrounding area. Mt. Esther provides a nice half-day trip from town or a scenic hiking detour from a car trip on Pikes Peak Highway.

GETTING THERE: From Colorado Springs, take US 24 west to the Chipita Park/ Green Mountain Falls exit. Take the left exit, bear left toward Chipita Park, and turn left onto Chipita Park Road. In 0.1 miles, turn right onto Picabo Road. Go up a steep hill for 0.4 miles and take a hard left just before you reach Mountain Road. Minimal parking is available along the side of the road. Look for a trail sign and stairs that mark the start of the hike. This drive is a challenge on a snowy winter day.

THE ROUTE: The trail ascends steeply on switchbacks, reaching a rock outcropping at 0.75 miles and a junction with the Ring the Peak Trail at 0.85 miles. The trail gains almost 1,000 feet in the first mile. Turn right at the junction and continue for 0.3 miles. The Ring the Peak Trail continues to the right; take the unmarked trail to the left and begin climbing the ridge toward the summit. Rock formations allow great views along both sides of the trail along this ridge. At 1.5 miles, reach the east summit. Scramble up the rocks on the left for 360-degree views, including the north face of Pikes Peak and the Bottomless Pit. Return via the same route.

Looking toward the west summit of Mt. Esther.   PHOTO BY GREG LONG

ALTERNATE ROUTE

An alternate approach to this peak is from the Crow Gulch Picnic Area on Pikes Peak Highway (toll). From Crow Gulch, hike a couple of hundred yards to an overlook with views of the peak and highway. Follow the trail and cross a creek at 0.2 miles and, at 0.7 miles, reach the junction where the standard route (described above) intersects with the Ring the Peak Trail.

SIDEBAR: RING THE PEAK TRAIL

The *Ring the Peak Trail* circumnavigates Pikes Peak. It is really a system of trails and connectors that, when put together, allow a user to travel approximately 63 miles around "America's Mountain," Pikes Peak, at elevations ranging from 6,400 to 11,400 feet.

Conceived in the 1990s and coordinated by the group "Friends of the Peak" (www.fotp.com), as of 2012 the trail system is about 80 percent complete and includes footpaths, dirt roads, and even a few paved roads. All segments of the trail are open to hikers, with most also being open to mountain bikers and equestrians. A few of the roads are accessible by four-wheel drive vehicles. The trail crosses or coincides with several of the trails in this guide, including Mount Esther, Barr Trail, the Heizer Trail, and the approach road to Almagre Mountain.

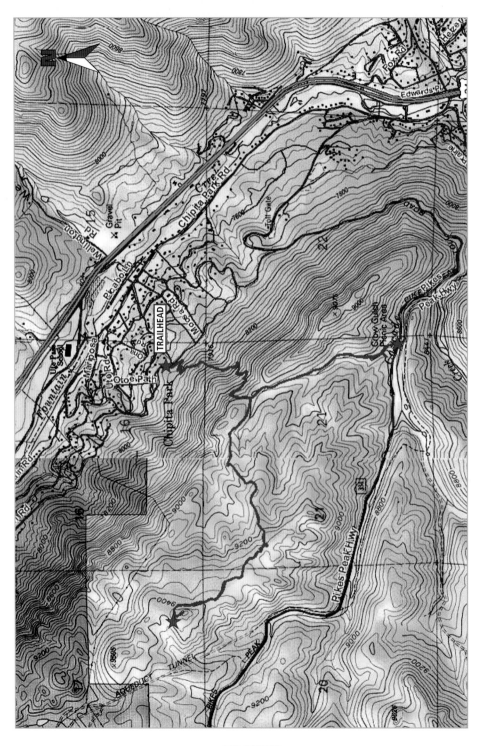

MT. ESTHER

15. Mueller State Park—Homestead, Beaver Ponds, Rock Pond Loop

BY DAN ANDERSON

MAPS	Trails Illustrated, Pikes Peak/Cañon City, Number 137 USGS, Divide; Cripple Creek North, 7.5 minute Trail Map from Mueller State Park
ELEVATION GAIN	950 feet
RATING	Moderate
ROUND-TRIP DISTANCE	5.8 miles
ROUND-TRIP TIME	3–4 hours
NEAREST LANDMARK	Divide

COMMENT: Mueller State Park has about 55 miles of trails and connects to additional trails in the Dome Rock State Wildlife Area, which borders the southwestern side of the park. Bikes and horses are not allowed on all trails, so check with the park service for rules. Snowshoeing and cross-country skiing are best after a good snowfall; otherwise, snow melts on the south-facing slopes, leaving the trails bare. Pets are not allowed on the trails.

A portion of the large campground is open in winter, and three cabins are available for rent year-round. The entry fee in 2012 was $7 per vehicle per day. An annual pass is available.

The park consists of rolling hills, forested ridges, grassy valleys, ponds, and interesting rock formations. Many groves of aspen trees offer spectacular fall color. There are great views of the west side of Pikes Peak and the Sangre de Cristo Mountains.

Horses and bikes are not allowed on Rock Canyon Trail and Revenuer's Ridge Trail. Horses and bikes are allowed on the Rock Pond Trail, Geer Pond Trail, and Lost Pond Trail. Bikes are allowed on Beaver Ponds Trail and Homestead Trail.

GETTING THERE: From Colorado Springs, take Interstate 25 exit 141 westbound on US 24 (Cimarron Street) toward Manitou Springs. Go 25 miles through Woodland Park to Divide. At the traffic light in Divide, turn left (south) on Colorado 67 and go 3.9 miles to the Mueller State Park entrance road. Turn right and go 1.6 miles to the turnoff into the parking lot for the visitor center.

THE ROUTE: This hike starts from the visitor center's parking lot. The main trailhead is at the far end of the parking lot from the visitor center. The other trailhead is not so obvious. The trail starts from the entrance road to the parking lot where the road branches to the back of the visitor center for park personnel. The Revenuer's Ridge Trail is accessed from here; this is also the end of the Wapiti Nature Trail. The hike described here ends at this trailhead.

Start at the far end of the parking lot where there are interpretive signs, a trailhead sign, and a sign identifying the Wapiti Nature Trail #6. The nature trail goes to the left and the Rock Pond Trail #5 goes to the right. Take the right fork downhill and cross the Wapiti Nature Trail in 0.13 miles. Continue to a horseshoe bend on a ridge where there is a large boulder to sit on and enjoy the great views. Pass by the junction of the Preacher's Hollow Trail #4 (which nosedives into a canyon) and reach the Four Mile Overlook #44 junction after 1.1 miles. This trail goes into the Dome Rock State Wildlife Area and is good for long hikes and remote country. The Rock Pond Trail branches to the right, dropping more steeply into the canyon where Brook Pond and Rock Pond are located. After 2.1 miles, there is a 0.22-mile side trip to Brook Pond. It is worth the trip, as this is one of the most picturesque ponds in the park.

After the trail junction to Brook Pond, continue another 0.13 miles down to Rock Pond. At Rock Pond, go across the dam and find the new (as of fall 2010) Rock Canyon Trail #15. This single-track trail goes up a narrow canyon, where a

Brook Pond, in Mueller State Park.   PHOTO BY DAN ANDERSON

Geer Pond, in Mueller State Park.

PHOTO BY DAN ANDERSON

bench is nestled among some boulders next to a small stream. This is a cool place to relax before the climb up the canyon.

The Rock Canyon Trail tops out at Geer Pond and, after 0.8 miles, reaches the junction of the Geer Pond Trail #25 and the Beaver Ponds Trail #26 on the north side of Geer Pond. Continue northward for 0.5 miles on the Beaver Ponds Trail #26, passing another junction of the Geer Pond Trail, climbing one short, steep grade to Homestead Trail #12. Turn right onto Homestead and follow it for 0.7 miles up to Revenuer's Ridge Trail #1 near the Homestead Trailhead.

Take Revenuer's Ridge Trail to the south (right) 0.4 miles to the Lost Pond Trail. Go past the spur to the Lost Pond Trailhead and around a curve. The wide trail goes straight ahead, becoming the Livery Trail #20 to the equestrian trailhead. A single-track trail, Revenuer's Ridge, branches to the right. Continue on this trail to the Outlook Ridge Trail. Turn left (east), and go to the trailhead sign at the Outlook Ridge Trailhead. The Revenuer's Ridge Trail continues to the south (right) at the trailhead sign. Pass the Wapiti Nature Trail junction and arrive at the visitor center parking area to complete this hike.

ALTERNATE ROUTE

This route can be shortened by turning right (east) at the junction of the Geer Pond Trail, the Beaver Ponds Trail, and the Rock Canyon Trail and hiking up the Geer Pond Trail to Lost Pond and eventually to Revenuer's Ridge. Then turn right on Revenuer's Ridge Trail and follow it to the visitor center.

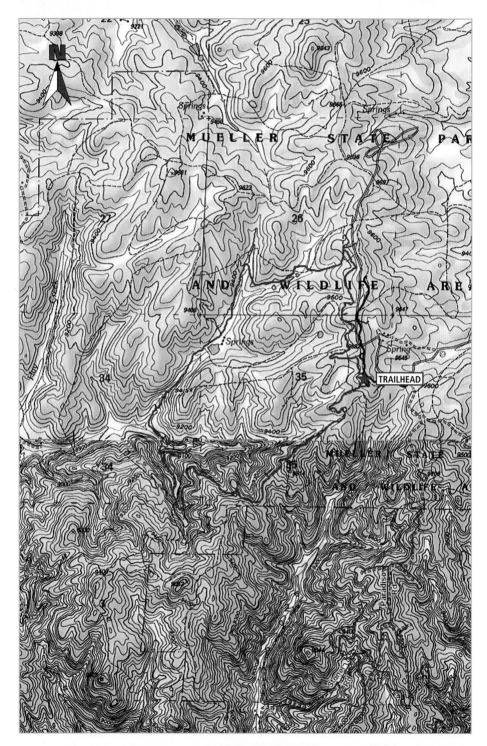

MUELLER STATE PARK

16. Paint Mines Interpretive Park

BY BILL HOUGHTON

MAPS	USGS, Calhan—1970
	El Paso County Parks Handout
ELEVATION GAIN	465 feet
RATING	Easy
ROUND-TRIP DISTANCE	4.1 miles
ROUND-TRIP TIME	1.5–2.5 hours
NEAREST LANDMARK	Calhan

COMMENT: The El Paso County Parks web page notes, "The Paint Mines are dominated by clays deposited more than 55 million years ago, and the surrounding acreage has yielded evidence of human life dating as far back as 9,000 years. American Indian tribes used this land as a favorite hunting ground where badland breaks and gullies may have served as hunting overlooks and entrapment locations for bison kill." A stroll through this park is a stroll through history as well as several different ecosystems.

GETTING THERE: The nearest town (Calhan) is 29 miles east of Colorado Springs from the intersection of Powers Boulevard and Colorado 24. From the eastern edge of Calhan, turn right (south) on Yoder Road. Note several signs pointing to the El Paso County Fairgrounds. Drive 0.6 miles south past the fairgrounds and turn left (east) on Paint Mines Drive. Go 1.4 miles east and then south to the north parking lot for the Paint Mines. To get a great perspective of the Paint Mines, continue to drive south beyond the parking lot to a small viewpoint for an overview.

THE ROUTE: This interpretive park lies just south of the town of Calhan. It is hard to consider driving this far away from the Front Range without thinking about the anomaly this area presents within the overall environment and the uses the area has been put to in the past. During the drive east from Colorado Springs, imagine the Plains Indians coming here to gather clay coloring for their pottery and painting themselves in ceremonial colors for their annual tribal rites.

Colorful hoodoos in Paint Mines Interpretive Park. PHOTO BY BILL HOUGHTON

The park itself emphasizes the two aspects of this environment in two loops. The first, or northern, loop is 1.6 miles long and represents the short grass prairie that dominates the whole environment. It is accessed by taking the left trail at the junction several hundred feet from the northern parking lot. To access the loop containing the paint mines, take the right trail at the junction to a central junction at an intermittent (usually dry) creek crossing. At the creek crossing, turn right (south) and follow the creek bed into the eroded areas. Different areas have different colors, but the total impression is like a bowl of rainbow sherbet. Be aware that this *is* a creek bed and may flood in a thunderstorm. Be sure to take the spur south to the head of the canyon. Please stay on the creek bed and do not climb onto the formations. If you return from the spur and get back onto the prepared trail, the loop continues past several minor erosive spots and into the prairie. It is 2.5 miles from the central junction back to that junction.

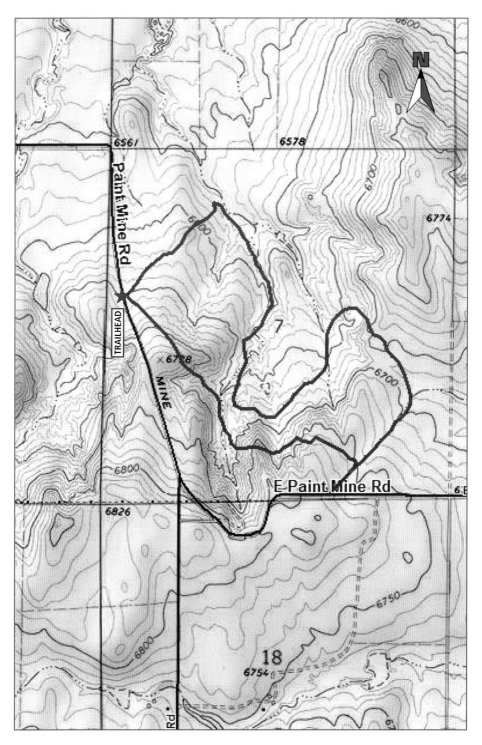

PAINT MINES INTERPRETIVE PARK

17. Pipeline Trail to Emerald Valley

BY GREG LONG

MAP	Trails Illustrated, Pikes Peak/Cañon City, Number 137
ELEVATION GAIN	600 feet
RATING	Easy–moderate
ROUND-TRIP DISTANCE	7.2 miles
ROUND-TRIP TIME	3–4 hours
NEAREST LANDMARK	The Broadmoor Hotel

COMMENT: The Pipeline Trail is what it sounds like: a trail along the route of old pipeline. The trail leads into a picturesque area known as the Emerald Valley, home of many wildflowers in spring and summer and changing aspens in the fall—a great spot for a picnic if there ever was one. The largely flat terrain makes this a good choice for families or those unused to the rigors of climbing at altitude.

GETTING THERE: From Interstate 25, take exit 140, Nevada /Tejon. The second light off the exit ramp is Nevada. Follow the signs for Colorado 115 South

Aspen grove.   PHOTO BY GREG LONG

Cascade along the Pipeline Trail.

and take exit 46, Lake Avenue. At the Broadmoor Hotel, bear right onto Lake Circle. Take the roundabout to head left on Mesa Drive. Mesa becomes Park Road, then becomes El Pomar Road. Follow the signs toward the Cheyenne Mountain Zoo. After 0.5 miles, turn right onto Old Stage Road. Check your odometer. Old Stage turns to dirt at 0.8 miles. Pass the Broadmoor stables at 5.6 miles, and turn left at 6.1 miles onto Forest Service Road 371 toward Emerald Valley Ranch. Follow this road 0.5 miles over a hill and look for a small parking space on the right next to a rock wall; pipe will be visible. There is only space for one to two vehicles.

THE ROUTE: The trail sets off and almost immediately passes the ruins of an old mine. Cross a bridge over a pleasant cascade before going straight at a trail junction. At 0.8 miles, go right at another trail junction. The sounds of birds and a babbling stream may greet you as the forest begins to open up with views of the surrounding granite cliffs. At 2.0 miles, a road comes in from the left. Stay straight here and make note of the surrounding landmarks; it is easy to miss this turn on the return hike and accidentally stay on the road. Stay left at the fork at 2.5 miles. The trail begins to run along a creek for a mile before turning sharply right and uphill. This is Emerald Valley; end your hike here and return the way you came.

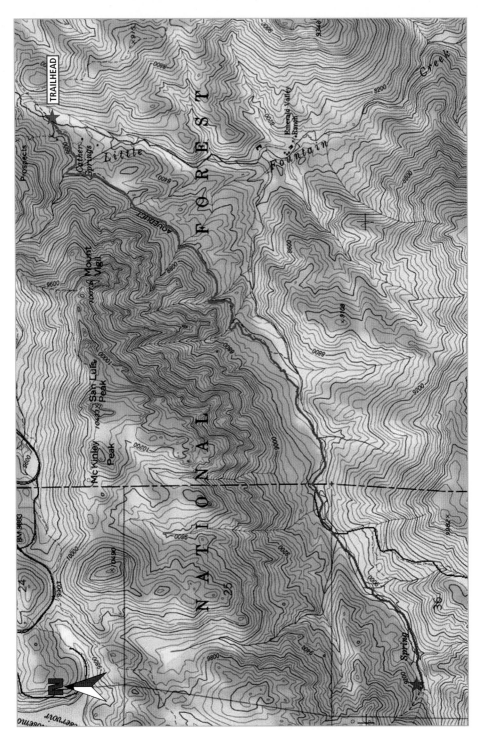

PIPELINE TRAIL

18. Stanley Canyon Trail

BY UWE K. SARTORI

MAPS	Trails Illustrated, Pikes Peak/Cañon City, Number 137 USGS, Cascade, 7.5 minute
ELEVATION GAIN	1,450 feet
RATING	Moderate
ROUND-TRIP DISTANCE	3.8 miles
ROUND-TRIP TIME	2–3 hours
NEAREST LANDMARK	Air Force Academy Hospital

COMMENT: The US Air Force Academy is a major landmark in the Colorado Springs area. Located on 18,000 pristine acres, the academy is home to the popular Stanley Canyon Trail and offers a wonderful three-season sample of the Pikes Peak area's eastern slope.

Enjoy a gentle hike beside a stream under an aspen canopy that leads into a meadow carpeted with alpine flowers, as well as steep hiking that gets the heart pumping. Challenge yourself by scrambling up granite rock. Soak in gorgeous vistas of the academy, the Black Forest area, and northern Colorado Springs—including towering granite outcroppings, alpine forests, and waterfalls. Count on varied flora and local wildlife to add color and excitement to your hiking experience.

The reward for your effort is the beautiful Stanley Reservoir. Here, you can relax and enjoy your time on the shoreline (no swimming allowed) before heading back down. Make this a day outing with a family picnic at the reservoir. Afterward, enjoy a tour of the academy grounds.

For the best experience, hike this trail between late May and early October. Late fall, winter, and early spring seasons bring winter conditions that make this trail potentially dangerous. This hike is not suitable for strollers or walkers. Mountain bikes are not recommended. The trail contains some steep, strenuous sections and requires a little scrambling.

As of late 2011, the Air Force was restricting access to this part of the academy grounds to those with military IDs. This policy has varied many times in the last few years and it is hoped that full access will open again.

Entering a meadow on Stanley Canyon Trail.

PHOTO BY UWE SARTORI

GETTING THERE: From Interstate 25, take exit 156B, N. Entrance/Air Force Academy. Be prepared to stop at the gate and show your ID. Drive 0.5 miles and go left onto Stadium Boulevard. Go 1.2 miles and turn right onto Academy Drive. Drive 2.4 miles and turn left onto Pine Drive. Go 0.2 miles and turn right onto an unmarked dirt road (just past the Air Force Academy hospital). Drive 0.6 miles to the trailhead. From the south entrance of the academy, drive north on South Gate Boulevard to Pine Drive. Turn left onto Pine Drive and travel 3.9 miles to the unmarked dirt road on the left. From this direction, you will almost certainly drive past the road; turn around when you get to the hospital.

THE ROUTE: Walk past the gate at the trailhead to the road. Shortly after starting up the road, take a left fork. Less than 75 yards after the fork, a sign directs you to the right. Walk another 100 yards and turn left at the next sign for Stanley Reservoir 707.

Be ready for a mile of steep, loose dirt and gravel on the trail. While ascending, first listen, and then look, for a small waterfall to the left. Further up, the trail will appear to overlap with a stream. Continue on, staying close and to the right of the stream. Resist the temptation to angle steeply up to the right as it leads off trail. Some sections give the opportunity to do a little scrambling on the granite rock. One short section involves hopping over rocks in the stream itself. Be careful: wet rock and wet boots make for a slippery climb.

After the first mile, the trail mellows into a gentle hike. Pass through a small meadow and into a tree-canopied section over a stream crossing, complete with a makeshift log bridge. Soon, cross the stream again. For the last 0.5 miles, enjoy the trail as it alternates between meadows and trees, finally winding its way through a large meadow to the bottom of the reservoir dam. From here, a short trail to the left brings you to the shore of the reservoir.

FURTHER INFORMATION

The Air Force Academy visitor hours are from 8:00 a.m. to 6:00 p.m. Some of the trail is on Air Force Academy property, which means you are subject to the academy's jurisdiction. The remainder of the trail and the reservoir are in Pike National Forest.

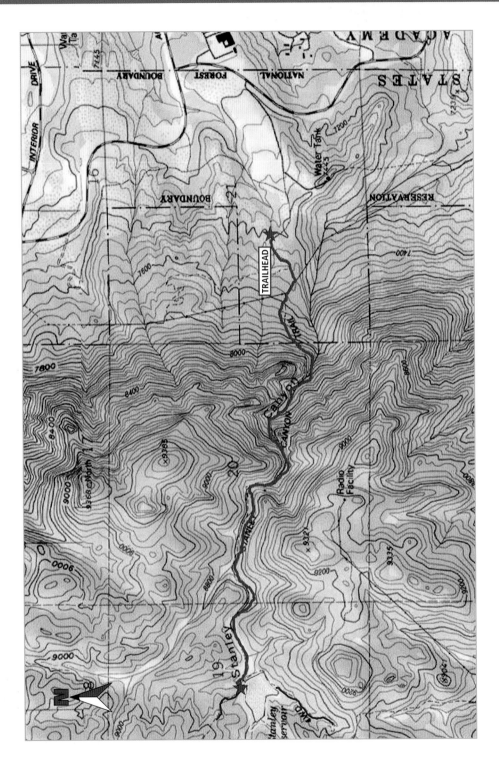

STANLEY CANYON TRAIL

19. Ute Valley Park

BY GREG LONG

MAP	Trails Illustrated, Pikes Peak/Cañon City, Number 137
ELEVATION GAIN	200 feet
RATING	Easy
ROUND-TRIP DISTANCE	2.3 miles
ROUND-TRIP TIME	1–1.5 hours
NEAREST LANDMARK	North Colorado Springs

COMMENT: Ute Valley Park is another gem in the City of Colorado Springs park system. Featuring over 5 miles of trail for hikers and mountain bikers as well as good bouldering for climbers, this park offers ample recreation opportunities on the north side of the city. The loop described is one of many possibilities; check out the variety of interconnected trails in this park.

An oasis of wilderness in Colorado Springs.   PHOTO BY GREG LONG

A bouldering challenge.

GETTING THERE: From Interstate 25, take the Woodmen Road exit 149 and head west. At 0.4 miles, Woodmen goes right; stay straight on Rockrimmon Boulevard for 1.8 miles to Vindicator Road (traffic light). Turn right on Vindicator and proceed 0.8 miles to the trailhead, a small parking area on the left just past Eagleview Middle School. The parking lot has room for about a dozen cars and has a port-a-potty.

THE ROUTE: Leave the lot on the wooden planking and bear left at the end of the planks to head up a small hill. Climb on a gravel path for about 0.5 miles, then descend, trading views of the back of the middle school for views of Pikes Peak, which dominates the skyline to the west. Cross a creek bed that may or may not be flowing, depending on the time of year. Turn left onto a sandy trail and in 10 yards turn right uphill. Cross over the hill, passing manhole covers, and turn right at the marked trail sign. At 1.4 miles, reach the southwest entrance of the park and turn right. Blodgett Peak and the peaks above the Air Force Academy come into view. At 2.10 miles, stay right on a wide path to return to the parking lot. The loop may be hiked in either direction.

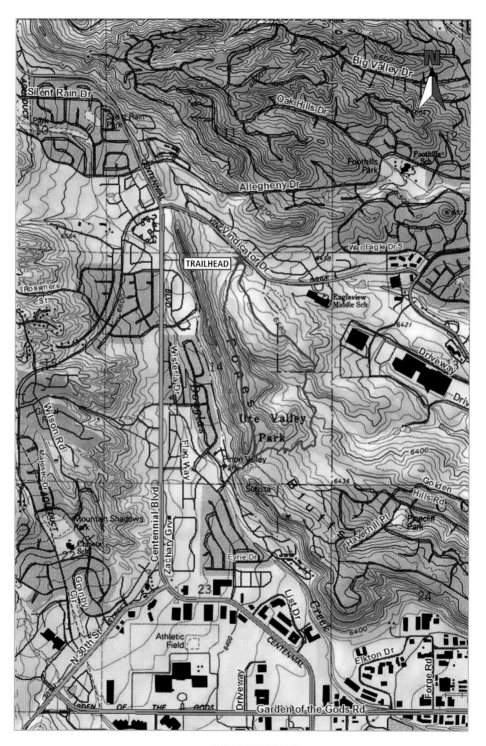

UTE VALLEY PARK

20. Waldo Canyon

BY GREG LONG

MAP	Trails Illustrated, Pikes Peak/Cañon City, Number 137
ELEVATION GAIN	1,350 feet
RATING	Moderate
ROUND-TRIP DISTANCE	6.9 miles
ROUND-TRIP TIME	3–5 hours
NEAREST LANDMARK	Manitou Springs

COMMENT: Waldo Canyon is possibly the most popular trail in the Colorado Springs area, and it deserves to be. With easy access from a state highway, great scenery, and moderate terrain, there is much to recommend this trail. It may be possible to have the trail to yourself if you hike it at night during a blizzard, but otherwise expect the company of other hikers, trail runners, and mountain bikers. This writer has hiked the trail many times and driven by it hundreds of times without ever seeing the parking lot empty. Don't go expecting solitude and you won't be disappointed; the hike is worth the sacrifice. [**NOTE:** As this guide went to press, a devastating wildfire swept through Waldo and Williams Canyons. It is likely that these trails will be closed for a period of time, and may deviate from these descriptions when re-opened. Please check for updated information before hiking.]

GETTING THERE: From Interstate 25 Colorado Springs, take Colorado 24 west for 7.3 miles to reach the trailhead, a pullout on the right side of the road. The pullout is around a blind corner, so look for a hiker sign just before the corner to warn of the turn. This lot can be crowded; some overflow parking can be found on the eastbound side of the highway.

THE ROUTE: Waldo is a "lollipop" trail with an out-and-back approach to a loop. The trail begins steeply up a set of stairs. After an overlook at 0.4 miles, the trail turns north away from the highway and the traffic noise decreases markedly. After 1.5 miles, descend into an open meadow and reach a bench and the beginning of the loop at 1.7 miles. The loop portion can be hiked either direction and is described counter-clockwise. Immediately, the climb gets

Rock formations near the trail's highpoint.

steeper, but the views of Pikes Peak easily compensate. At 2.2 miles, the grade moderates and sandstone cliffs join Pikes Peak in the viewshed. The trail stays relatively flat with gentle ups and downs for the next 0.75 mile before climbing again to its highpoint at 8,150 feet—almost exactly halfway through the hike at 3.4 miles. Descend into forest and a creek crossing at 4.0 miles. At 4.3 miles, follow the signs and turn left at the trail junction. Return to the bench and the start of the loop at 5.2 miles, and then back down to the trailhead.

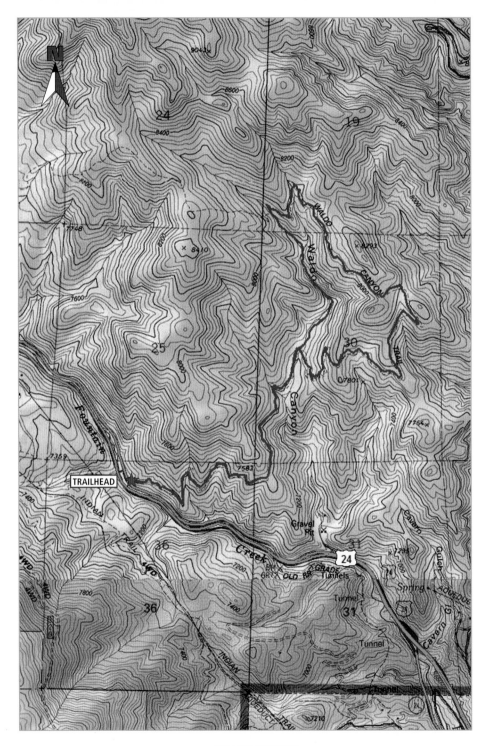

WALDO CANYON

21. Williams Canyon

BY BILL BROWN

MAPS	Trails Illustrated, Pikes Peak/Cañon City, Number 137; Pikes Peak Atlas
ELEVATION GAIN	900 feet (1,400 feet with the Waldo connector)
RATING	Easy–moderate
ROUND-TRIP DISTANCE	4 miles (5.4 miles with the Waldo connector)
ROUND-TRIP TIME	2–3 hours
NEAREST LANDMARK	Manitou Springs Post Office

COMMENT: Talk about close to home! This hike can easily be walked from downtown Manitou Springs. The description begins a few blocks north of Manitou Avenue. The route features limestone bluffs, an intermittent waterfall and stream, and an optional link to the Waldo Canyon loop.

The hike goes through the private property of Cave of the Winds. The gate and sign near the mouth of the canyon intimidate many and probably inhibit use of the trail. However, the owners permit hiking in Williams Canyon for anyone who signs a liability waiver and files it with the Cave of the Winds office in the nearby visitor center. Waivers are kept on file for one year. The waiver form may also be found at www.inclineclub.com/caveofthewinds.pdf but must be filed in person at the visitor center.

The trail crosses the stream about 15 times each way. During late summer and fall it may be completely dry. In spring and early summer the stream is likely flowing, sometimes at considerable volume, making these crossings tricky. Icy conditions are the norm in winter, and there is seldom enough snow for snowshoeing.

Williams Canyon is popular with cavers; you may notice their social trails climbing either side of the canyon and even some cave openings. Expert mountain bikers occasionally use the trail, climbing Rampart Range Road through Garden of the Gods then riding the technical downhill through Williams Canyon. [**NOTE:** As this guide went to press, a devastating wildfire swept through Waldo and Williams Canyons. It is likely that these trails will be closed for a period of time, and may deviate from these descriptions when re-opened. Please check for updated information before hiking.]

GETTING THERE: From Interstate 25, take exit 141 (US 24/Cimarron Street) west for 5 miles to Manitou Springs. Turn left at the *Cliff Dwellings Road* sign on the US 24 bypass, proceed down the hill for 0.3 miles, turn right at El Paso Boulevard for 400 feet, and turn right onto Manitou Avenue. Go 0.2 miles; bear right onto Canon Avenue. Go 0.2 miles and again bear right at the stop sign, staying on Canon Avenue. Continue for 0.2 miles; park near the *Local Traffic Only* and *No Outlet* signs at the intersection of Canon Avenue and Glenn Road.

THE ROUTE: The first 0.9 miles of the hike are on the old exit of Cave of the Winds, abandoned as a roadbed in about 1990. Walk northwest on Canon Avenue, and in 100 yards pass under the US 24 bypass. Pass a few residences whose architectural style might be labeled "Manitou eclectic." At mile 0.25, approach the gate and sign; continue through it if you've filed a liability waiver at Cave of the Winds. At mile 0.6, the Cave of the Winds visitor center comes into view atop the limestone cliffs on your left. The road ends and the hike abruptly takes

Looking south past cliffs.   PHOTO BY BILL BROWN

Rock spires along the trail.

PHOTO BY BILL BROWN

on a more natural character at mile 0.9. The single track trail passes through Douglas fir, gambel oak, and a few cottonwoods.

At mile 1.2 the trail begins to climb over some scree and rock outcrops to an overlook. There's a nice view down the canyon to the south, a (seasonal) waterfall, and a couple of smooth bathtub pools. Continue following the trail up the canyon and several creek crossings. For the purposes of this description, the trail ends at a side drainage to the west at mile 2.0. Retrace your steps to the trailhead, watching for several windows and arches in the limestone bluffs that may be more easily spotted on the way down.

ALTERNATE ROUTE

From the turnaround point at mile 2.0 the hiker has two additional options. The trail up the side drainage to the west connects with the Waldo Canyon loop. This option adds 0.7 miles and 500 feet of elevation. The trail continuing to the north climbs to Rampart Range Road in about 1.0 miles and 600 feet. A US Forest Service outdoor shooting range is about 0.25 miles from the intersection of this trail and the road. This shooting area was closed in 2008 and its future is uncertain. If gunfire is heard, the trail extension (northward beyond mile 2.0) should be avoided altogether.

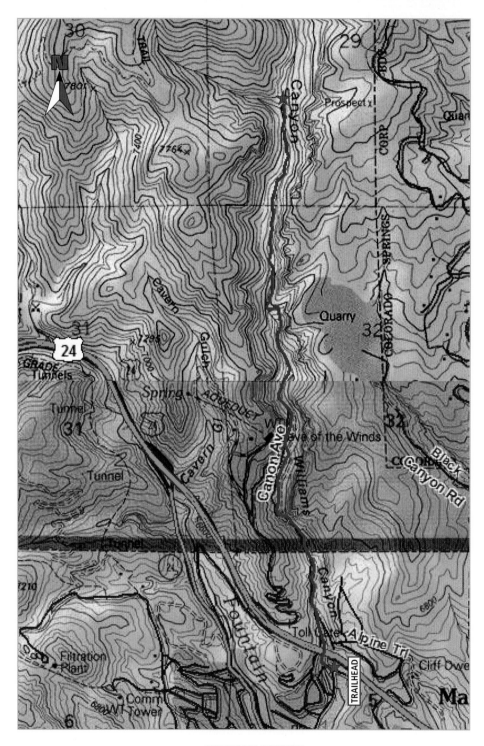

WILLIAMS CANYON

22. Arkansas Point

BY BILL BROWN

MAPS	Lake Pueblo State Park (Colorado State Parks)
	South Shore Trails of Lake Pueblo SP (Western Maps LLC)
ELEVATION GAIN	350 feet
RATING	Easy
ROUND-TRIP DISTANCE	2.2 miles
ROUND-TRIP TIME	1–1.5 hours
NEAREST LANDMARK	Lake Pueblo State Park Visitor Center

COMMENT: This is not a mountain hike, or even a foothills hike; it is a desert hike. Its arid character makes a unique contribution to the Southern Front Range landscape.

The route climbs to a rocky ridge with a scenic overlook of Lake Pueblo, its dam, and South Shore Marina. It makes a good choice for a fall, winter, or early spring outing. Summer can be brutally hot. You may share some sections of trail with mountain bikers and equestrians.

The cholla cactus is not your friend. Its stems are very tenuously attached to the rest of the plant, and its spines are full of microscopic barbs. The slightest brush with the cholla can result in its sticking to skin or clothes and a very painful process of removing it. It's sometimes called the "jumping cholla" because it seems to jump through the air to embed itself in your skin if you get anywhere near it.

Take time to check out the visitor center, which features interpretive exhibits of the flora, fauna, and geology of the region. It also offers an interesting account of the massive Frying Pan/Arkansas project, which diverts water from the western slope across the Continental Divide to the Arkansas River.

GETTING THERE: From the north, take Interstate 25 exit 101. Go west on US 50 for 2.5 miles. Turn south on Pueblo Boulevard (Colorado 45) for 3.8 miles. Turn west on Thatcher Avenue (Colorado 96). Follow Thatcher (which bends southwest) for 3.8 miles. Turn right (northwest) at the entrance sign for Lake Pueblo. This is South Marina Road; follow it for 0.9 miles and turn south into the Arkansas Point Campground parking lot. Along the way, stop to purchase a state park pass, currently $7 per vehicle, at either the gatehouse or the visitor center.

From the south, take Interstate 25, exit 94. Go west on Pueblo Boulevard (Colorado 45). Pueblo Boulevard bends northward; stay on it for 4.6 miles. Turn west on Thatcher Avenue (Colorado 96), and continue as above from Thatcher Avenue.

Another approach from the south is to follow Thatcher (which bends southwest) for 3.8 miles and turn right (northwest) at the entrance sign for Lake Pueblo. This is South Marina Road; follow it for 0.9 miles and turn south into the Arkansas Point Campground parking lot.

THE ROUTE: The hike begins at the small covered shelter with trail information and a bench. It is a few steps west of a public restroom. Look a few yards to the south and find an unsigned single-track trail leading left off the main

Cholla along the trail.   PHOTO BY BILL BROWN

A wide open trail near Arkansas Point. PHOTO BY BILL BROWN

South Shore Trail. Follow this trail 0.2 miles to access the Conduit Trail. Turn left (east) on Conduit. At mile 0.3 (past the turnoff for Staircase Trail), turn right on Steep Tech Trail. This intersection does not currently have a sign, but it may be marked by a small pile of rocks. This section climbs southeast, gradually at first, then more steeply. Landscape timbers reinforce some of the bigger steps. The trail allows close contact with the shale barrens and sedimentary bluffs that make up the mesa.

Top out at mile 0.6, where the trail meets the Arkansas Point Trail. Enjoy the views of the reservoir as you walk west along a rocky ridge. The trail ends at mile 0.75. From here retrace your steps and continue east a few steps beyond the Steep Tech Trail. Go right (southwest) at the signed Water Tower Trail. Follow the gully filled with shale ledges down to an abandoned water tank and beyond. Watch for a trail that bears right at mile 1.7. This is the Conduit Trail; follow it around the base of the Arkansas Point ridge you were on earlier. Turn left at mile 2.0 to return to the trailhead.

Take time to survey the extensive network of trails along the ridges and through the canyons to the south. These hold promise of further exploration of Lake Pueblo's South Shore trails.

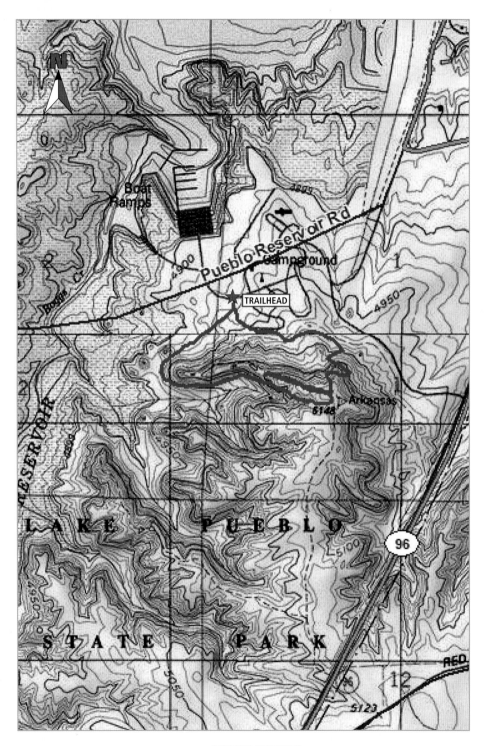

ARKANSAS POINT

23. Bushnell Lakes

BY GREG LONG

MAP	Trails Illustrated, Sangre de Cristo/Great Sand Dunes NP, Number 138
ELEVATION GAIN	4,200 feet
RATING	Moderate–difficult
ROUND-TRIP DISTANCE	9.2 miles
ROUND-TRIP TIME	7–9 hours
NEAREST LANDMARK	Coaldale

COMMENT: The Bushnell Lakes sit high in the Sangre de Cristos in a large cirque. Check out the many visible rock layers and cascading waterfalls, and enjoy the sun glistening on the water and the green grass and bushes juxtaposed

Enjoying lunch by the lower lake.   PHOTO BY GREG LONG

Entering the wilderness.

against the gray rock. When approaching the lake, Bushnell Peak looms above on the left and South Twin Sister is on the right.

GETTING THERE: Take US 50 West to the town of Coaldale. Turn left onto County Road 6, Hayden Creek Road. Drive toward Hayden Creek Campground. After about 4.5 miles, begin to look for parking along the road. The trail begins in the campground, but parking is only available for those spending the night.

THE ROUTE: From the campground sign, cut through the first campsite to the bridge over Hayden Creek and the intersection with the Rainbow Trail. Climb steadily for 2.5 miles on rocky trail to a trail junction. The sign indicates the Rainbow Trail, but not the cross trail. Turn left on the cross trail and in 100 feet reach the registration sign to enter the Sangre de Cristo Wilderness. At this point, the trail becomes foot traffic only. For the next mile, the trail climbs more steeply through aspens and on looser rock. The trail reaches a ridgeline and flattens out briefly before descending slightly into a cirque on scree. Climb again to reach lower Bushnell Lake at 4.6 miles. Enjoy a stop here or continue on the upper lakes. On the descent, be sure to watch for the fork leading right, back to Hayden Campground.

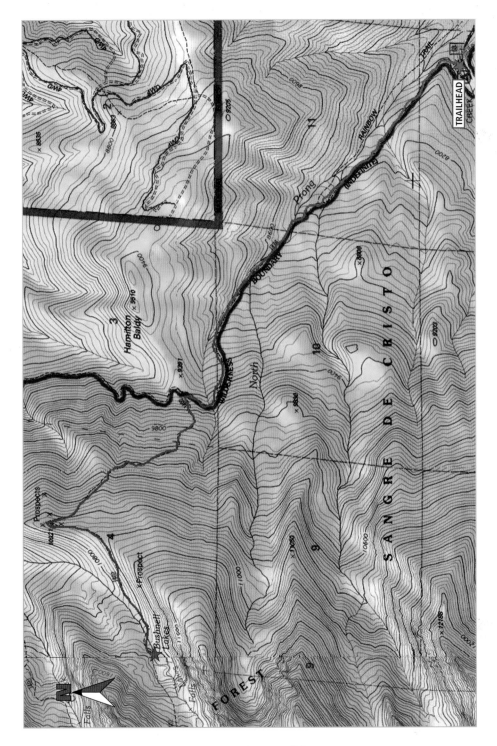

BUSHNELL LAKES

24. California Peak

BY GREG LONG

MAPS	Trails Illustrated, Sangre de Cristo/Great Sand Dunes NP, Number 138
ELEVATION GAIN	4,100 feet
RATING	Difficult
ROUND-TRIP DISTANCE	8.2 miles
ROUND-TRIP TIME	8–10 hours
NEAREST LANDMARK	Walsenburg

COMMENT: At 13,849 feet, California ranks as a Centennial, one of the hundred highest peaks in Colorado. It gets far less traffic than the nearby Fourteener, Mt. Lindsey, and the fairly moderate terrain can make hiking it a pleasant, if long, day. Be forewarned, almost half the distance of this hike is above treeline and exposed to all the weather Colorado can dish out. Be sure to get a very early start to avoid summer's afternoon thunderstorms.

Fall colors around Lost Lake.   PHOTO BY GREG LONG

Approaching the summit of California Peak.

PHOTO BY GREG LONG

GETTING THERE: A high-clearance, four-wheel-drive vehicle is recommended to get to this trailhead. From Interstate 25, take exit 52 toward Walsenburg. In 0.4 miles, turn right onto Colorado 69. Take 69 23.3 miles to Gardner; pass through Gardner and turn left toward Redwing. At 7 miles from this turn, the road becomes dirt; at 11.4 miles, turn left toward Upper Huerfano and Lily Lake. At 15.5 miles, pass the Singing River ranch. The road becomes rougher at this point. At 19.8 miles, reach the trailhead. Look for a sign indicating the Zapata Trail and Huerfano Trail. This is the Lower Huerfano Trailhead. There is a small parking area at the sign, with room for more cars a little further up the road.

THE ROUTE: Follow the Zapata Trail (853) for 1.8 miles as it climbs, steeply at times, through forest then open meadow before reaching the northwest ridge of California Peak. The trail may be faint at times, so pay close attention. When in doubt, aim for the ridge. Once on the ridge, turn left (south) and ascend the grass slopes toward the summit. Enjoy views of the surrounding high peaks as well as the Great Sand Dunes National Park in the distance. Cross a false summit, point 13,476, and descend before climbing back to the true summit. Enjoy views of Fourteeners from the summit: to the south is Blanca, with Little Bear peeking out behind it; Lindsey is to the southeast.

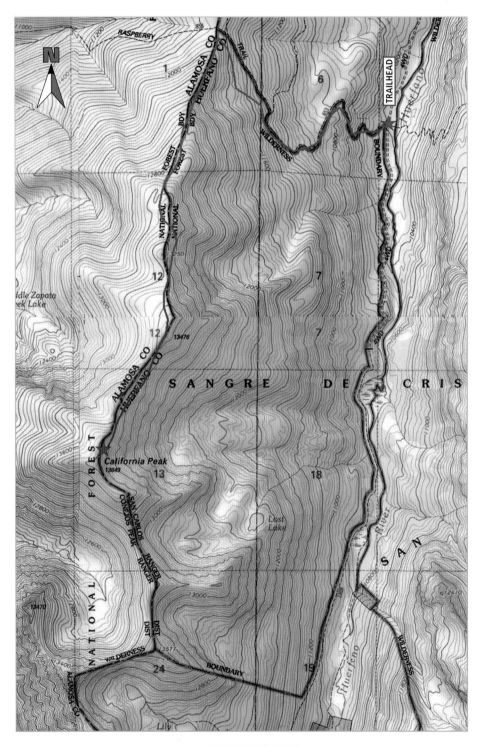

CALIFORNIA PEAK

25. Comanche-Venable Loop

BY DAN ANDERSON

MAPS	Trails Illustrated, Sangre de Cristo /Great Sand Dunes, Number 138 USGS, Rito Alto Peak, Horn Peak, 7.5 minute
ELEVATION GAIN	4,000 feet
RATING	Difficult
ROUND-TRIP DISTANCE	12 miles
ROUND-TRIP TIME	9–12 hours
NEAREST LANDMARK	Westcliffe

COMMENT: For an introduction to the Sangre de Cristo ("Blood of Christ") Mountains, this is an excellent hike. Most of the hike is in the Sangre de Cristo Wilderness and offers spectacular scenery, lakes, abundant wildflowers, and vast stands of aspens for great fall color.

The beginning and end of the hike use part of the Rainbow Trail. This is a motorized trail, so all-terrain vehicles and motorcycles may be encountered. Rainbow Trail is more than 100 miles long, extending along the eastern side of the range by wrapping around the north side to the west side, where it crosses US 285 near Marshall Pass Road.

GETTING THERE: From the junction of Colorado 96 and Colorado 69 in West-cliffe, head south on Colorado 69 (Sixth Street) and go 3.4 miles to County Road 140 (Schoolfield Road). Watch for signs to the Alvarado Trailhead and the Alpine Lodge. Turn right (west) and go 4.6 miles to a "T" intersection with County Road 141 (Willow Lane). Turn left (south) and go 0.2 miles to where the main route turns right (west), and continue 1.7 miles to a junction. At this junction, the Alvarado Campground and Alpine Lodge are straight ahead. Turn right and go 0.4 miles up a series of switchbacks to the Alvarado Trailhead parking area.

From the south side of Pueblo, take Interstate 25 exit 94 westbound on Colorado 45 (West Pueblo Boulevard). Go west 2.3 miles to South Pueblo Boulevard. Continue north 2.5 miles on South Pueblo Boulevard to Thatcher Avenue (Colorado 96). Turn left (west) on Colorado 96 and go 25.9 miles to Wetmore and the junction of Colorado 96 and Colorado 69. Follow the directions above from Wetmore to the Alvarado Trailhead.

THE ROUTE: From the west side of the Alvarado Trailhead parking area, follow the trail uphill and southwest past the upper campsites of Alvarado Campground. The trail heads west and crosses the Rainbow Trail then climbs relentlessly up the east side of Spring Mountain through beautiful stands of aspens and conifers. As the top of an eastern ridge of Spring Mountain gets closer, this part of the climb finishes with 10 switchbacks. Cross the ridge at 11,040 feet into the Hiltman Creek drainage, where Comanche Lake is located. The trail continues the climb at a gentler angle on the south side of Spring Mountain. Here the views of the canyon are superb.

After 3.9 miles, a short spur trail branches left to the outlet of Comanche Lake at 11,650 feet. Most hikers will want to take a break here and enjoy the views.

From Comanche Lake, it is 1.4 miles and 1,160 feet to the pass, making this the steepest segment. Early in the season, snow banks and cornices can make this pass difficult and dangerous to reach. If you are hiking this loop in the counter-clockwise direction, the trail crosses the ridge to the east side about 40 feet uphill and north of where the trail comes to the edge from the west.

The next stop is a pass east of Venable Peak. It is 0.9 miles away on a nearly flat trail. After this pass, the trail moves along a narrow shelf called Phantom Terrace. The shelf is typically 3 to 4 feet wide, with a few spots nearer 2 feet wide

The Venable Creek Trail.   PHOTO BY DAN ANDERSON

The Sangre de Cristo Range looms in the distance.   PHOTO BY DAN ANDERSON

because of a steeper slope on the outer edge. Early season snow banks or late-season ice flows from water seepage make this segment of the trail treacherous.

After crossing Phantom Terrace, watch for a trail junction about 0.6 miles from the pass where this route switchbacks down the hill. The trail straight ahead goes to Venable Pass. It is about 0.5 miles down to Venable Lakes and then 0.7 miles down to the lower ponds, which will soon be meadows. There you will find many campsites and the ruins of a cabin. It is a nice place to stop for a break.

From here the trail drops deeper into the canyon with conifer forests and, later, aspen groves. After 1.4 miles and just after a switchback, a spur trail leads to Venable Falls. The falls rush down a long cascade in a chasm and are worth seeing.

Continue down the trail from Venable Falls for 1.9 miles to the junction of the Rainbow Trail. Turn right (southeast) and go 160 feet to another trail junction. Turn left to leave the Rainbow Trail and go 0.5 miles back to the Alvarado Trailhead.

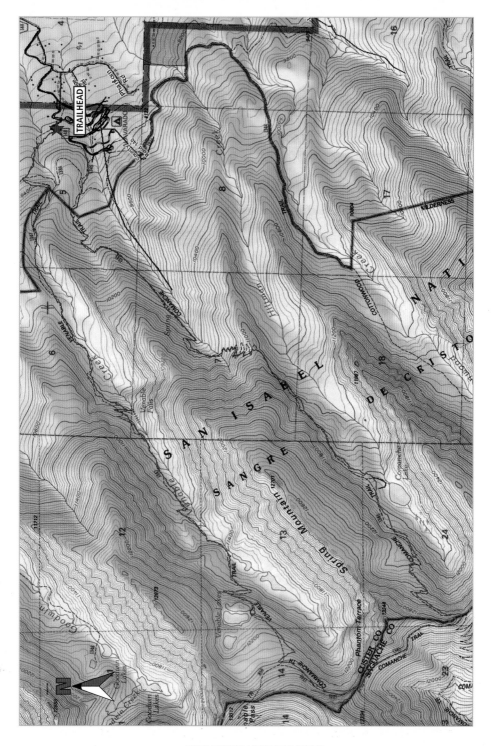

COMANCHE-VENABLE TRAIL

26. Curley Peak

BY GREG LONG

MAP	USGS, Curley Peak
ELEVATION GAIN	2,300 feet
RATING	Moderate
ROUND-TRIP DISTANCE	6.80 miles
ROUND-TRIP TIME	3–5 hours
NEAREST LANDMARK	Cañon City

COMMENT: Curley Peak resides in a trail system just south of Cañon City, making it a great short outing from that town or a worthy day trip from other areas. The peak can be climbed directly from either the Stultz Trail or Tanner Trail and can be included in loop hikes with Tanner Peak if a car shuttle is available. The dramatic rock formations combine with views west to the Sangre de Cristo Range to make this area worth spending a day. One caveat is that the trail is also

The Sangre de Cristos can be seen along the trail.　　　　　　PHOTO BY GREG LONG

Views through the trees.

popular with motorized users on dirt bikes. Saving this hike for winter may provide a quieter and more enjoyable experience.

GETTING THERE: Take US 50 to Cañon City and turn left at Ninth Street. In a mile, when Colorado 115 heads left, turn right onto Elm Avenue. Go 0.25 miles and turn left onto Oak Creek Grade Road. Check your odometer. Pass the Tanner Trailhead at North Cow Creek at 4 miles, pass the Stultz Trailhead at 8 miles, and reach the southern end of the Tanner Trail at the East Bear Gulch Trailhead at 10.5 miles. Park in the large area on the left side of the road.

THE ROUTE: Cross the road to the trail and climb through forest and over some downed trees. Reach a plateau at 2.0 miles and begin to see the Sangres in the distance along with rock formations in the foreground. Continue up to a ridge at 9,400 feet and hike north for about a mile to the junction with the Stultz Trail. From this junction, Curley Peak is an off-trail scramble south over rocks. Once on top, take in views of the Sangre de Cristos to the west and Pikes Peak to the north. Tanner Peak is visible along the ridgeline to the north.

If a car shuttle is available, it is possible to continue along the Tanner Trail all the way to Tanner Peak and down to North Cow Creek for an all-day, 13.5-mile loop. Loops are also possible using the Stultz Trail to descend from Curley Peak.

CURLEY PEAK

27. Dry Creek Trail

BY GREG LONG

MAP	Trails Illustrated, Sangre de Cristo/Great Sand Dunes NP, Number 138
ELEVATION GAIN	2,700 feet
RATING	Moderate–difficult
ROUND-TRIP DISTANCE	8.5 miles
ROUND-TRIP TIME	5–7 hours
NEAREST LANDMARK	Westcliffe

COMMENT: Yes, the name may be oxymoronic, but the hike is stunning. The Dry Creek Trail leads to a series of three lakes set in a high basin in the Sangre de Cristo Wilderness. Yes, they have water in them. They are also surrounded by the rugged summits of Horn, Little Horn, and Fluted peaks. This trail makes for a great day hike; if a weekend backpack trip is desired, ample campsites around the lakes make it an excellent option as well.

GETTING THERE: From the junction of Colorado 69 and Colorado 96 in West-cliff, drive south on County Road 69 for 3.3 miles and turn right on Schoolfield

Fluted Peak rises above the Dry Lakes.   PHOTO BY GREG LONG

Dry Lakes from above.

Road. Go 0.7 miles and turn left on County Road 125, then go 1.7 miles and turn right onto County Road 130. Proceed 3.9 miles to the trailhead; look for a sign and an outhouse.

THE ROUTE: From the trailhead, hike a spur trail 0.6 miles to connect with the Rainbow Trail and turn right. Pass the trail to Horn Creek Lakes at 0.7 miles and the Horn Creek spur at 1.1 miles, and reach the signed junction with the Dry Lakes Trail at 1.3 miles. Turn left and start up the trail. The trail winds its way, climbing moderately along the creek, sometimes approaching it and sometimes meandering away before crossing it at 2.0 miles. Continue to climb steadily for another two miles to reach the sign marking the wilderness boundary. Here the trail rises steeply and breaks out above treeline for the last quarter mile to the lower lake. Enjoy views of the surrounding peaks ringing the basin. When the light is right, the rock formations reflected in the water can be truly amazing to behold. There is no established trail to the upper lakes, so be prepared for some rough travel to gain the upper basin, or just hang out at the lower lake and enjoy a nice lunch and the well-earned views.

It is possible to climb Horn Peak by ascending to the second lake, and then up the slopes toward the saddle on the ridge between Horn and Fluted. The direct ascent from the lower lake is steep with loose rock, and is not recommended.

On the return hike, it will be tempting to turn off on the Horn Creek Spur. Be sure to wait and take the second spur trail to return to the correct parking area.

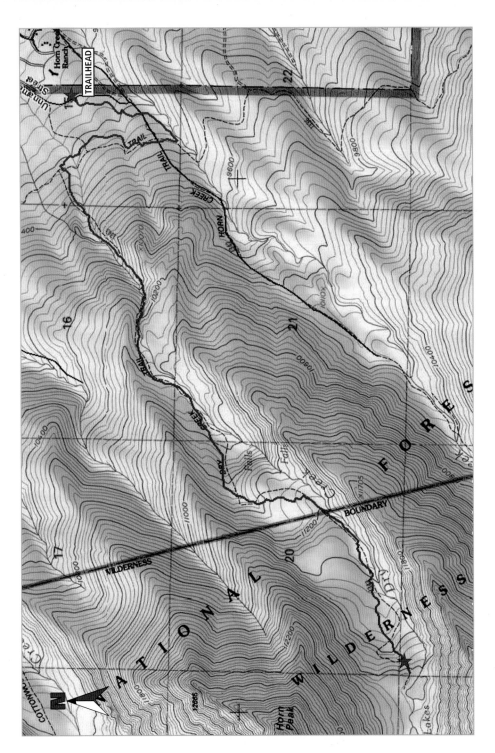

DRY CREEK TRAIL

28. Goodwin Lakes Trail

BY DAN ANDERSON

MAPS	Trails Illustrated, Sangre de Cristo Mountain/Great Sand Dunes, Number 138 USGS, Rito Alto Peak, Horn Peak, 7.5 minute
ELEVATION GAIN	2,700 feet
RATING	Moderate
ROUND-TRIP DISTANCE	10.4 miles
ROUND-TRIP TIME	5–7 hours
NEAREST LANDMARK	Westcliffe

COMMENT: The east side of the Sangre de Cristo Mountains has many side canyons with picturesque lakes at the base of high rugged mountains. The base of the range is around 9,000 feet and several lakes are near timberline, 11,500 feet, or higher. Numerous mountain passes are over 12,000 feet. Trails up the canyons gain elevation quickly, giving the hiker a good workout.

Goodwin Lakes Trail goes up one of these canyons to a couple of lakes near timberline and a third lake above timberline. June brings wonderful displays of wildflowers at lower elevations and snow banks as timberline is approached. July brings out even more wildflowers, especially at higher elevations.

Many trails up the side canyons follow parts of what were once roads. These make for wide trails but also for rocky trails, as they serve as channels for water runoff. The trails become less rocky at higher elevations.

The beginning and end of the hike use part of the Rainbow Trail. This is a motorized trail, so all-terrain vehicles and motorcycles may be encountered. The Rainbow Trail is more than 100 miles long, extending along the eastern side of the range, wrapping from the north side to the west side, where it crosses US 285 near the Marshall Pass Road. Motorcycles and bicycles are not allowed on most of the side trails because they are in the Sangre de Cristo Wilderness.

GETTING THERE: From the intersection of Colorado 96 and Colorado 69 in Westcliffe. Turn south onto Colorado 69 (Sixth Street) and go 3.4 miles to County Road 140 (Schoolfield Road). Watch for signs to the Alvarado Trailhead and the Alpine Lodge. Turn right (west) and go 4.6 miles to a "T" intersection with County Road 141 (Willow Lane). Turn left (south) and go 0.2 miles to where

Taking a break at Lower Goodwin Lake.   PHOTO BY DAN ANDERSON

the main route turns right (west), and continue 1.7 miles to a junction. At this junction, the Alvarado Campground and Alpine Lodge are straight ahead. Turn right and go 0.4 miles up a series of switchbacks to the Alvarado Trailhead parking area.

THE ROUTE: From the north side of the Alvarado Trailhead parking area, head north for 0.5 miles to the Rainbow Trail junction, crossing a bridge over Venable Creek along the way. Turn right here and go 160 feet to the Venable Trail junction. Continue ahead on the Rainbow Trail for 0.9 miles to the Goodwin Lakes Trail junction and turn left.

Proceed up the Goodwin Lakes Trail for 3.4 miles to the lower Goodwin Lake. The upper Goodwin Lake is another 0.4 miles on a primitive trail. The stream from the upper lake to the lower forms a picturesque cascade with a beautiful display of wildflowers.

Along the way notice what may be a glacial terminal moraine with a meadow on the uphill side. The meadow may once have been a lake.

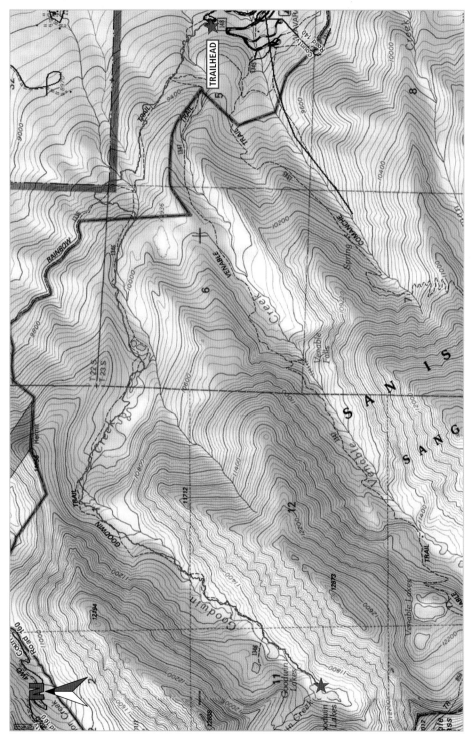

GOODWIN LAKES TRAIL

29. Greenhorn Mountain
(12,347 feet)

BY GREG LONG

MAPS	USGS, Rye, San Isabel
ELEVATION GAIN	1,000 feet
RATING	Moderate
ROUND-TRIP DISTANCE	Greenhorn round trip = 5.2 miles Greenhorn and North = 5.7 miles Greenhorn with return via Bartlett Trail = 5.0 miles Greenhorn and North with return via Bartlett Trail = 5.5 miles
ROUND-TRIP TIME	3–5 hours
NEAREST LANDMARK	Rye

COMMENT: Greenhorn Mountain is the highest point in its namesake wilderness and the Wet Mountains. It provides spectacular above-treeline views without a significant expenditure of effort. Take advantage of the many campsites along the road in and make a weekend of this beautiful and relatively untraveled part of the state. There are a variety of trails in the area and many great views of the Sangre de Cristo Mountains and the Spanish Peaks. This entire trail is above treeline; watch for afternoon lightning storms and use extreme caution in bad weather.

GETTING THERE: From Interstate 25, take exit 74, Colorado 165. Go through Colorado City and Rye, and pass Bishop's Castle. After a hairpin turn, turn left onto Forest Service Road 360, Ophir Creek Road (dirt). This road is labeled Forest Service Road 400 on some older maps. At 7.5 miles, turn left onto Forest Service Road 369. Continue another 15.5 miles to the trailhead. The last mile is a little rough, but the road is passable in passenger cars.

THE ROUTE: Leave the trailhead on good trail and work up to the saddle, gaining more than half the elevation in the first mile. At the saddle, you have the choice of turning left and climbing 200 feet to the summit of the northern sub-

Spanish Peaks in the distance.   PHOTO BY GREG LONG

peak on grass and talus. To reach the main summit, follow the ridgeline to the right over several gentle ups and downs. The true summit is the furthest point along this ridge. Enjoy views of Pikes Peak to the north, the Crestones to the west, and the Spanish Peaks to the south.

Return the way you came, or drop south of the summit to connect with the Bartlett Trail, which traverses the base of the peak. The descent off the summit is on steep, loose rock and is not for the faint of heart. Turn right when you reach the trail to return to the parking lot.

SIDEBAR: BISHOP'S CASTLE

Started by owner Jim Bishop in 1969, Bishop's Castle is a unique and fascinating site. It is, in short, a castle on the side of the road. Jim Bishop has built it entirely by hand. It is free and open to the public (donations accepted) and well worth a stop on your way to or from the peaks in this area.

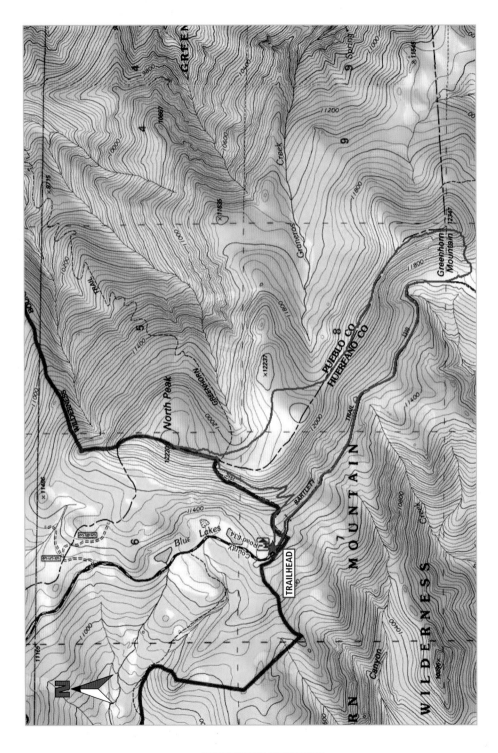

GREENHORN MOUNTAIN

30. Horn Peak

BY GREG LONG

MAP	Trails Illustrated, Sangre de Cristo/Great Sand Dunes NP, Number 138
ELEVATION GAIN	4,300 feet
RATING	Difficult
ROUND-TRIP DISTANCE	10.6 miles
ROUND-TRIP TIME	7–10 hours
NEAREST LANDMARK	Westcliffe

COMMENT: While the Fourteeners and high Thirteeners get all the publicity and the traffic, peaks like Horn Peak provide beauty and challenge without all the crowds. It is not unusual for climbers to have the summit of this peak all to themselves, where they can take in views of the nearby Fourteeners.

GETTING THERE: From the junction of Colorado 69 and Colorado 96 in Westcliffe, drive south on 69 for 3.3 miles and turn right on Schoolfield Road. Go 0.7 miles and turn left on County Road 125, then 1.7 miles and turn right onto County Road 130. Proceed 3.9 miles to the trailhead; look for a sign and an outhouse.

Breaking out above treeline.   PHOTO BY GREG LONG

Crestone Peak and Needle viewed from the summit.

THE ROUTE: From the trailhead, hike a spur trail 0.6 miles to connect with the Rainbow Trail and turn right. Pass the trail to Horn Creek Lakes at 0.7 miles, the Horn Creek Spur at 1.1 miles, and the Dry Lakes Trail at 1.3 miles before turning left on the Horn Peak Trail at 1.9 miles. Now the fun begins. The first half mile is steep and moves steadily up a wide, rocky trail. Enter the Sangre de Cristo Wilderness, cross Hannequin Creek (may be dry) at 3.1 miles, and climb a series of switchbacks up to the ridge. There are many social trails in this area; be sure to stay on the main trail. Break out of the trees at 4.2 miles and work your way toward the false summit. The trail becomes faint above treeline, so look for posts that mark the way. When in doubt, aim for the crest of the ridge.

Crestone Needle looms large in the distance as you reach the sub-peak at 12,700 feet. Stay left and below the ridgeline to traverse the last half mile and climb the final 700 feet to the true summit. Enjoy great views, including five of the hundred highest peaks in Colorado right in a row: From left to right, they are Humboldt Peak, Crestone Needle, Crestone Peak, Kit Carson, and Mt. Adams.

Descend via the way you came or—for an adventurous alternative—via the Dry Creek Trail. To connect with the Dry Lakes, descend the southwest ridge of Horn all the way to the saddle before dropping down to the upper Dry Lake. While it is possible to drop more directly down the gullies near the summit, these are steep with considerable loose rock and are not recommended.

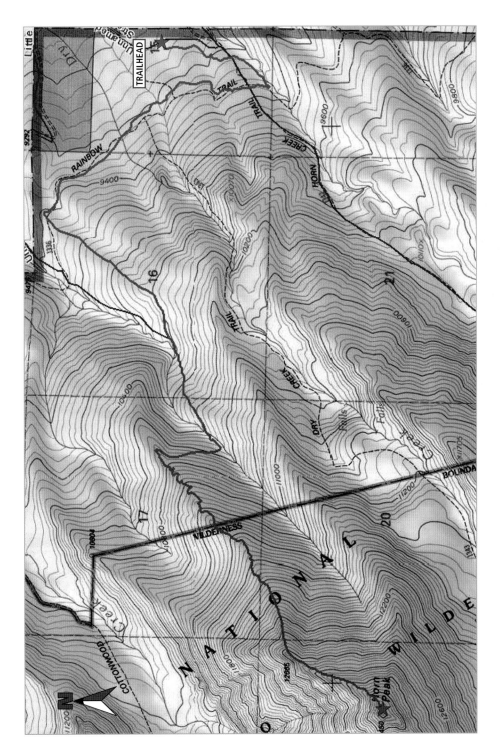

HORN PEAK

31. Lily Lake

BY GREG LONG

MAP	Trails Illustrated, Sangre de Cristo/Great Sand Dunes NP, Number 138
ELEVATION GAIN	1,700 feet
RATING	Moderate
ROUND-TRIP DISTANCE	6.8 miles
ROUND-TRIP TIME	3–4 hours
NEAREST LANDMARK	Walsenburg

COMMENT: The Sangre de Cristo Range is deservedly well known for its high 13,000- and 14,000-foot mountains, but beneath those mountains are myriad cirques containing pristine high mountain lakes with views of the peaks above. One such cirque contains Lily Lake and makes an excellent day trip or weekend backpack.

GETTING THERE: A high-clearance, four-wheel-drive vehicle is recommended to get to this trailhead. From Interstate 25, take exit 52 toward Walsenburg. In 0.4 miles, turn right onto Colorado 69. Take 69 23.3 miles to Gardner; pass

Blanca Peak.   PHOTO BY GREG LONG

Peaks above Lily Lake.   PHOTO BY GREG LONG

through Gardner and turn left toward Redwing. At 7 miles from this turn, the
road becomes dirt; at 11.4 miles turn left toward Upper Huerfano and Lily Lake.
At 15.5 miles, pass the Singing River Ranch. The road becomes rougher at this
point. At 19.8 miles, pass the Lower Huerfano Trailhead, and continue 2.1 more
miles to the Upper Huerfano, aka Lily Lake, Trailhead. The last mile of road is
particularly rough.

THE ROUTE: From the parking lot, follow the Lily Lake Trail for 1 mile—the
first mile coincides with the trail up Mt. Lindsey, and you may have some peak-
baggers for company as you start out—and turn right to stay on the trail. Turn
right again in a quarter mile. Enjoy the waterfalls as you approach the lake, and
then view Blanca's north face once you arrive. At the lake, kick back and enjoy
the views or scramble around on the nearby boulders. A really hot day might
lead the truly daring to take a dip.

It is possible to ascend California Peak from Lily Lake. From the end of
the lake, scramble north up talus and scree slopes. This scramble may be
loose, and prudent climbers may desire a helmet. Connect with the ridge just
short of Point 13,577. Enjoy views of Lost Lake and east to the plains as you
traverse the ridgeline over a sub-peak to the summit of California. Return the
way you came or by reversing the ascent route of California, hike # 24 in this
book.

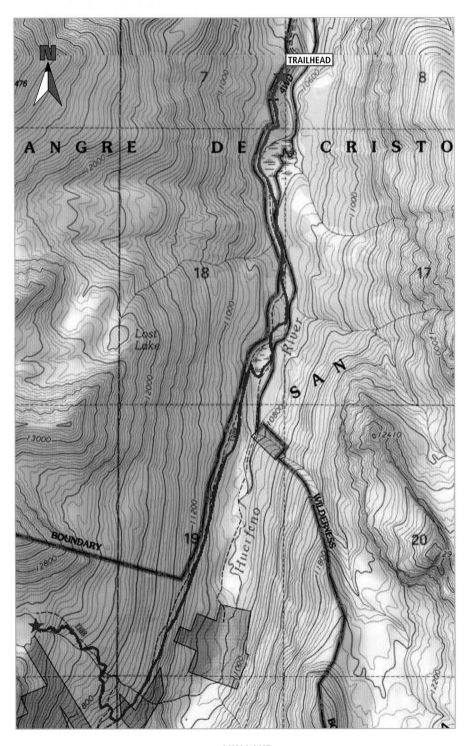

LILY LAKE

32. Mount Lindsey

(14,042 feet)

BY GREG LONG

MAP	Trails Illustrated, Sangre de Cristo/Great Sand Dunes NP, Number 138
ELEVATION GAIN	3,400 feet
RATING	Difficult
ROUND-TRIP DISTANCE	8.0 miles
ROUND-TRIP TIME	8–10 hours
NEAREST LANDMARK	Walsenburg

COMMENT: While certainly not Colorado's easiest Fourteener, Mt. Lindsey is the easiest Fourteener in the Sangre de Cristos and sees a fair amount of hiker traffic on weekends. Given the sometimes loose rock near the summit, it is usually best to be among the first climbers on a given day.

GETTING THERE: A high-clearance, four-wheel-drive vehicle is recommended to get to this trailhead. From Interstate 25, take exit 52 toward Walsenburg. In 0.4 miles, turn right onto Colorado 69. Take 69 23.3 miles to Gardner; pass through Gardner and turn left toward Redwing. At 7 miles from this turn, the road becomes dirt; at 11.4 miles, turn left toward Upper Huerfano and Lily Lake. At 15.5 miles, pass the Singing River Ranch. The road becomes rougher at this point. At 19.8 miles, pass the Lower Huerfano Trailhead and continue 2.1 more miles to the Upper Huerfano, aka Lily Lake, Trailhead. The last mile of road is particularly rough.

THE ROUTE: Follow the Lily Lake Trail for a mile until it turns right toward the lake. Continue straight at this turn. The trail from this point is not well developed and can be hard to follow at times. Continue along the trail and cross to the east side of the Huerfano River. Continue south on the trail as it begins to climb out of the river valley toward a boulder field. Cross a creek and enjoy views of Blanca looming ahead with Lindsey's summit just coming into view above you. Ascend on switchbacks to a ridge at 13,000 feet, and head east to meet the main ridge between Lindsey and the Iron Nipple. Follow the ridge and look for cairns

A hiker begins the summit ridge.

PHOTO BY DOUG HATFIELD

leading left (east) of the ridgeline to a rock gully; climb the gully on loose rock as it leads back to the summit ridge and an easy traverse to the summit. For those with the skills for exposed class-three scrambling, the loose rock can be avoided by staying on the main ridgeline all the way to the summit.

From the top, enjoy excellent views of (from left to right) Little Bear, Blanca, Ellingwood Point, and California along with the plains stretching out to the east. A fall hike of this peak can yield fantastic aspen-viewing opportunities.

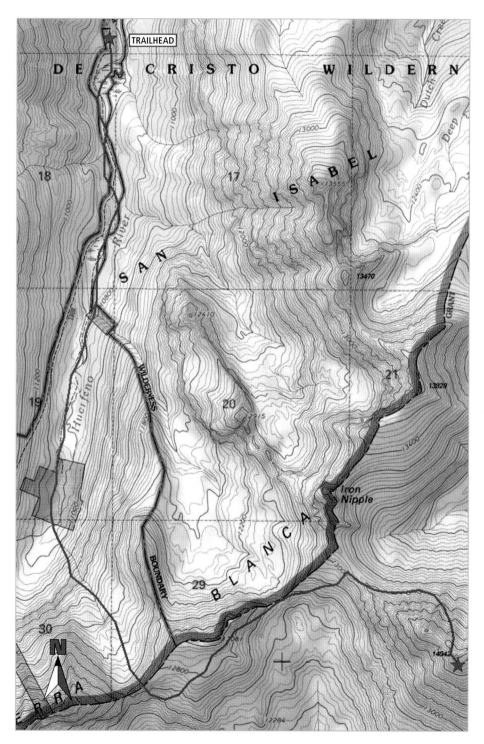

MT. LINDSEY

33. Newlin Creek Trail

BY ERIC SWAB AND DEBRA BLOCH

MAPS	USGS, Rockvale, CO 7.5 minute map (shows road to trailhead but not the trail)
ELEVATION GAIN	1,300 feet
RATING	Easy–moderate
ROUND-TRIP DISTANCE	6.0 miles
ROUND-TRIP TIME	4 hours
NEAREST LANDMARK	ADMAX Prison

COMMENT: The Newlin Creek Trail takes the hiker into a beautiful narrow canyon in the Wet Mountains. For the history buff, there is a reward at its end. The canyon is forested with white fir, Douglas fir, Ponderosa pine, Rocky Mountain juniper, aspen, gambrel oak, and a rich assortment of undergrowth. The granite cliffs and spires that line the stream attract technical climbers. Because of the tree cover along the entire trail this can be a comfortable hike even in hot weather. To protect the Greenback Cutthroat Trout, fishing in Newlin Creek is prohibited.

GETTING THERE: From Interstate 25 take exit 101 and drive west on US 50 for 24.5 miles. Take the exit for Colorado 115 to Florence and drive 4.8 miles; turn left at the first traffic light on Colorado 67. Drive 4.4 miles to County Road 15 and turn right. A sign here says *Newlin Cr Tr, No. 1335 6.5* [miles]. In 3.6 miles this paved road turns to gravel. The road forks twice; take the right fork each time, following the signs to Florence Mountain Park. As you pass a brown house on the left, the road narrows to a single lane, turns to dirt, and dead ends into the trailhead parking.

THE ROUTE: The trail starts at the west end of the parking area. A large part of the trail follows a nineteenth-century logging road. Where the old road has been washed out a good trail has been constructed. The tread of the trail is rocky, so good shoes or boots are recommended. About 0.5 miles up the trail is a picnic table. A little further on is the first and only bridge. There are 17 stream crossings in all; none are difficult. At the fourth crossing, the stream forks. The trail follows the right fork, which generally carries less water than the left fork trail

Cliffs above Newlin Creek Trail.

does. At 1.8 miles you will enter an aspen grove. At 3 miles you will find the nearly complete sawmill erected by Nathaniel Herrick in 1887.

Still to be seen are the steam boiler and the steam engine complete with flying ball governor and flywheel. Lying on the ground just north of the boiler is the smoke stack, and just east of the boiler is what was probably an auxiliary water tank. Be sure to look for the cast iron face on the boiler. About 260 feet north of the boiler, hiding off to the left of the trail, is a stone fireplace and chimney.

The official Trail No. 1335 ends here. There is an unofficial trail that climbs steeply to the top of the ridge; however, it is not recommended.

These remains are protected by federal law. Please take only pictures.

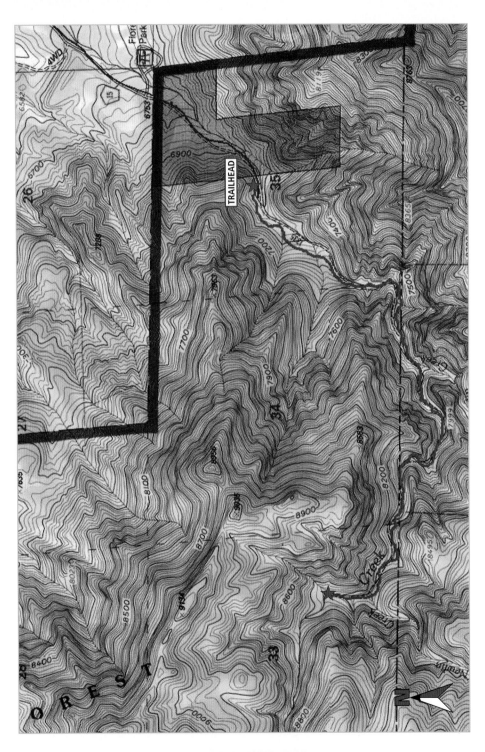

NEWLIN CREEK TRAIL

34. Pueblo Riverwalk

BY BRITTANY NIELSON

MAP	Pueblo Bicycle and Trails Map
ELEVATION GAIN	0 feet
RATING	Easy
ROUND-TRIP DISTANCE	1.1 miles
ROUND-TRIP TIME	30 minutes
NEAREST LANDMARK	Pueblo Convention Center

COMMENT: The Historic Arkansas Riverwalk of Pueblo is a great location for a leisurely walk in the heart of this historic city. The riverwalk is paved and is bordered by several restaurants, making it nice for an after-dinner walk or stroll with kids. This location is home to many local events, including a farmer's market in the summer and a lighting event for Christmas.

The riverwalk was dedicated in 2000. It was constructed to memorialize a major flood on the Arkansas River on June 5, 1921. The flood, caused by cloudbursts, came through on a Friday evening, and emergency personnel were given a 30-minute warning. Police were able to evacuate some during this time, but the flood still resulted in the loss of more than 100 lives. Old newspaper articles state the downtown area was buried in 10 feet of water and the railroad yard sat under 15 feet of water. An odd accompaniment to the flooding was fire caused by burning timber from a flaming lumberyard floating through the downtown area. The flood left mud, destruction, debris, and a loss of services and communication for several days. The only access into Pueblo from Colorado Springs was across a railroad bridge that was deemed unsafe after the flood. Reporters did not obtain accurate information for days as even they refused to cross this bridge.

The riverwalk is in the heart of the downtown shopping district among both historic and modern buildings. A walk through this park includes many memorials, a veterans' bridge, and numerous friendly ducks.

GETTING THERE: Exit Interstate 25 at First Street in Pueblo, exit 98B. Go west down the hill and take the third left onto Union Street. Union is approximately 0.75 miles west of I-25, and this intersection does not have a traffic light. Drive just under another 0.75 miles on Union. Cross a bridge and observe an oval, red-brick

Riparian area below the Riverwalk.   PHOTO BY BRITTANY NIELSON

building on the right. Once over the bridge, begin looking for parking along the road. If no parking is available, take the first right on D Street and take another right into a public parking area. Park near the large red-brick warehouse.

THE ROUTE: From the parking area, walk beyond the warehouse toward the water. Follow the ramp down to the water and head to the right. This area has the highest concentration of food options available, including a coffee shop, a snack shop, and an Italian kitchen. Also consider visiting options on the other side of the riverwalk, near the end of the walk described here.

After approximately 0.2 miles, follow the walk as it meanders along the water, which branches off to the right. Walk approximately 0.1 miles more and cross the bridge to the left. From here you will have a great view of a natural riparian environment. Continue turning back to the left, walk along the road for less than 0.1 miles, and turn left on the walk to head back toward the water.

Continue along the walk and arrive back at the split with the water. Continue on the walk down the opposite branch. When the waterway ends near the convention center, turn left and keep turning left to arrive on the other side of the waterway. Continue along the waterway, and pass under Veterans' Bridge. This bridge is dedicated to all veterans in the Pueblo area, and a kiosk under the bridge lists their names. Walk back by the restaurants and bars observed earlier, go back under Union Bridge, and wrap around past Kelly Falls to the start of the walk.

PUEBLO RIVERWALK

35. Rainbow Trail

BY GREG LONG

MAP	Trails Illustrated, Sangre de Cristo/Great Sand Dunes NP, Number 138
ELEVATION GAIN	1,100 feet
RATING	Easy
ROUND-TRIP DISTANCE	3.8 miles
ROUND-TRIP TIME	2–3 hours
NEAREST LANDMARK	Coaldale

COMMENT: The Rainbow Trail runs most of the length of the Sangre de Cristo Range for 100 miles between Salida and Westcliff. Most trails in the range intersect it at some point. The Rainbow Trail is a multi-use trail, and you may end up

This open meadow makes a great picnic spot.   PHOTO BY GREG LONG

Views along the trail.

sharing it with dirt bikes or all-terrain vehicles. It is usually best to divert onto side trails to avoid the sounds and smells of motorized use. This brief "sampler" describes a short hike along the trail to an open meadow with great views of the surrounding peaks—a beautiful spot for a picnic lunch.

GETTING THERE: Take US 50 West to the town of Coaldale. Turn left onto County Road 6, Hayden Creek Road. After 4.5 miles, bear left toward the Rainbow Trail and park.

THE ROUTE: Hike south on the Rainbow Trail. Cross a bridge after 0.6 miles and begin to climb steadily on switchbacks. The views begin to open up after a mile or so. At 1.75 miles, the trail starts to flatten out and the meadow opens up. Pick a good picnic spot anytime in the next quarter mile.

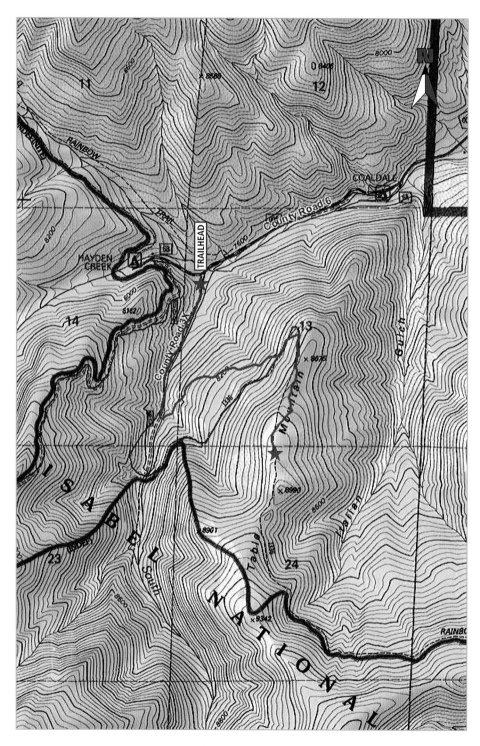

RAINBOW TRAIL

36. St. Charles Peak

BY ERIC SWAB

MAP	USGS, Saint Charles Peak, 7.5 minute map
ELEVATION GAIN	2,840 feet
RATING	Moderate
ROUND-TRIP DISTANCE	9.25 miles
ROUND-TRIP TIME	5.5–6.5 hours
NEAREST LANDMARK	San Isabel

COMMENT: The St. Charles Trail leads through a lush forest of aspen, Douglas fir, limber pine, white fir, Colorado spruce, and bristlecone pine. The terrain is steep, but the trail is well designed with lots of switchbacks, which make for a consistent, steady climb. The trail is open to hikers, equestrians, mountain bicycles, and motorcycles. All-terrain vehicles are not allowed. Motorcycles have created some trail damage at the higher elevations. Dogs must be "under control."

This is a good wildflower hike in the spring and early summer. Look especially for showy daisy, wild lily of the valley, false Solomon seal, twisted stalk, pyrola, monks hood, larkspur, yellow paintbrush, bush cinquefoil, and fireweed. Other than a few springs, there is no significant source of water, so carry what you need with you. Much of the trail is rocky with roots, so good shoes or boots are recommended. There are no side trails, but in a couple spots the trail is vague, so a map and compass or good route-finding skill is recommended.

GETTING THERE: From Interstate 25, take exit 74 toward Colorado City. This will put you on Colorado 165, which will take you to the trailhead. About 10 miles from I-25 the highway begins to climb into the Wet Mountains; at 17.5 miles you will pass Lake Isabel and a little further the town of San Isabel. At 21.7 miles you will find the trailhead parking on the right, or northeast, side of the road. The trailhead is directly across the highway from the parking.

THE ROUTE: The trail starts in a small valley but quickly climbs to a ridge top, which it follows for about 0.4 miles. You come to a small stream, which you follow, climbing above it until you reach a saddle at about 1.4 miles. Beyond the saddle the trail loses about 70 feet of elevation before you start to climb again to the second saddle at 2.9 miles. The trail is a little vague here and appears to fork;

Rocks along St. Charles Trail.

saddle the trail loses about 70 feet of elevation before you start to climb again to the second saddle at 2.9 miles. The trail is a little vague here and appears to fork; stay left on a compass heading of 240 degrees, and the trail will soon become obvious again. If you find yourself going downhill, you have missed the trail.

At 3.6 miles you will be on a ridge top where you can see a summit at compass heading of 210 degrees. You will climb this summit, but it is not St. Charles. In another third of a mile the view opens up to the Wet Valley and the Sangre de Cristo Mountain Range. Westerly, at compass bearing 260 degrees, you will see the triple summits of Humboldt, Crestone Peak, and Crestone Needle. In winter this part of the trail can be hidden by snow; however, substantial wooden posts mark the corners of each switchback. Follow them to the top of a ridge, where you will be among some beautiful bristlecone pines. Here for the first time you will see a bit of St. Charles' bald head peeking above the trees. In another 0.4 miles you will be rounding the northwest shoulder of St. Charles. The trail does not go to the top, so at the log portal on the right of the trail, turn left and walk up the gentle slope to the summit. Your reward is the 360-degree view. To the north is the Pikes Peak Massif; northeast is the Sawatch Range; west is the Sangre de Cristo Range; southeast are Blanca Peak, Little Bear Peak, and Mt. Lindsey; and just a little east of south are the Spanish Peaks.

The trail continues beyond this point to Greenhorn Mountain Road, Forest Service Road 369, which you can see below. That part of the trail is not included in this hike. Once you have soaked in all the panorama you can hold, return the way you came.

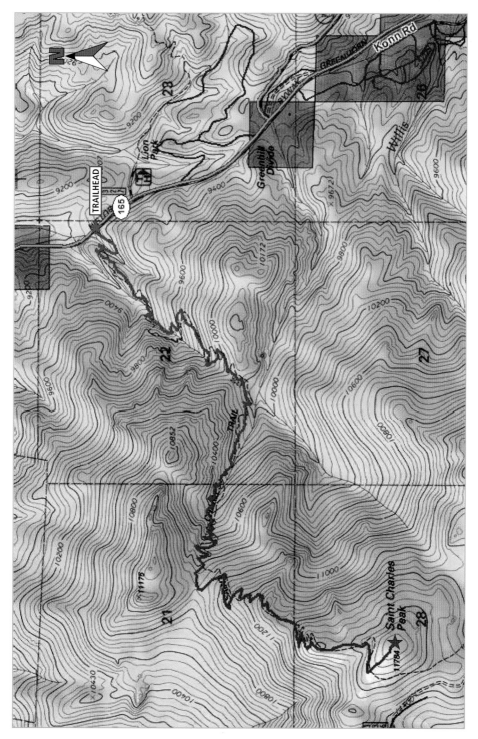

ST. CHARLES PEAK

37. Tower Trail—
Pueblo Mountain Park

BY GREG LONG

MAP	USGS, St. Charles Peak
ELEVATION GAIN	600 feet
RATING	Easy
ROUND-TRIP DISTANCE	1.8 miles
ROUND-TRIP TIME	1–1.5 hours
NEAREST LANDMARK	Pueblo

COMMENT: The Pueblo Mountain Park Environmental Center advertises having "something for everyone," and it certainly does. The park has 611 acres and miles of easy to moderate trails, along with nature programs, a visitor center, and an overnight lodge. The park was originally owned by the City of Pueblo. It was purchased by a nonprofit organization in 1999, which took over the park's management from the city in 2008. The park features ballfields and picnic areas with pit toilets. It is open from sunrise to sunset, and the visitor center is open from 8:00 a.m. to 4:00 p.m. The Horseshoe Lodge, a renovated 1930s building,

View from the fire tower.   PHOTO BY GREG LONG

Fire tower and picnic shelter.

is available for overnight stays and group retreats. Visit the web page www. hikeandlearn.org for details.

GETTING THERE: From Interstate 25, take exit 94 to Pueblo Boulevard. Go west for 2.8 miles to Northern Avenue and turn left. Northern Avenue becomes Colorado 78. Go about 23 miles to Beulah, to a fork in the road. Go left at the fork, and go 2.6 miles to the main entrance of the Pueblo Mountain Park, on the right. Enter the park and follow the sign to Horseshoe Lodge.

THE ROUTE: The Tower Trail is a short—but steep—climb to a fire tower and lookout. The top features a sheltered area and stairs to the tower, with 360-degree views of the park and surrounding area. Follow the trail through scrub oak and spruce for 0.6 miles. Turn left at the junction and continue for 0.3 miles to the summit.

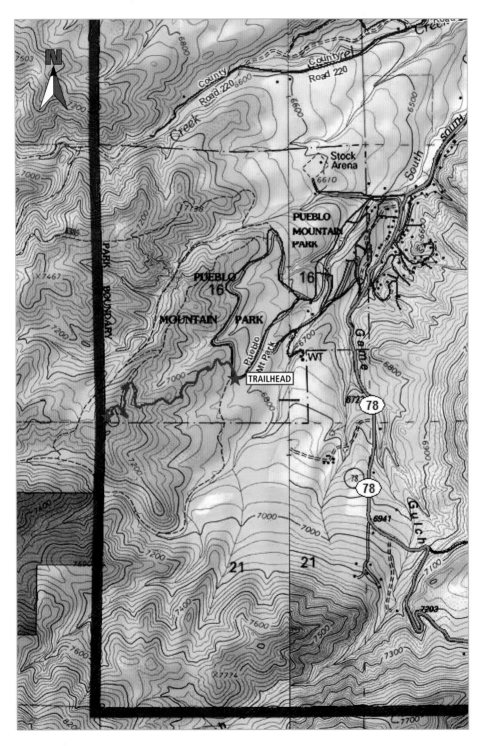

TOWER TRAIL

38. Apishapa Trail

BY BILL HOUGHTON

MAPS	US Forest Service, San Isabel National Forest USGS, Spanish Peaks, 1994 Herlick Canyon, 1994
ELEVATION GAIN	1,646 feet
RATING	Moderate
ROUND-TRIP DISTANCE	10.2 miles
ROUND-TRIP TIME	2–4 hours
NEAREST LANDMARK	Cucharas Pass

COMMENT: The Apishapa Trail is a great connector. It meets the Wahatoya Trail on the east end and is coincident with the West Spanish Peak Trail on the west. These connections provide several options for traversing any length from 5 miles to 17 miles of trail on the south side of the Spanish Peaks. It is a great trail for a morning's or afternoon's hike, or a full day if you so choose. Enjoy the unique geology of the area and the views of the Spanish Peaks, or take a picnic lunch in an open meadow.

GETTING THERE: Off of Colorado 12 (Highway of Legends) at Cucharas Pass, just south of the 22-mile marker, turn east onto a dirt road designated Huerfano County Road 346 (if you can find a highway sign). Most signs point to Cordova Pass, which is the western trailhead, so follow them. Cordova Pass is 6.1 miles east of the turnoff. Should you desire to hike up this trail, the eastern trailhead is another 5 miles down the same dirt road, which is now designated County Road 46. The elevation gained is from the eastern trailhead, and an equal amount would be lost coming from Cordova Pass.

THE ROUTE: This description assumes a start from the east trailhead. If you wish to start from Cordova Pass, just reverse the descriptions and mileage. The trail from the east trailhead starts out from a nice turnout parking area with room for 4–6 cars parked carefully. The trail starts north and in about 0.1 miles crosses County Road 46 and continues north to the sign-in and wilderness boundary. A well-established trail continues north through aspen and fir with some areas of moss hanging from the Douglas fir. Several of the famous igneous

Enjoying the view from Apishapa Trail.

PHOTO BY BILL HOUGHTON

dikes come into view. The hike gains almost half its total elevation in the first 1.5 miles to the trail intersection with the end of the Wahatoya Trail. Wahatoya goes east (right) and Apishapa goes west (left). Cross the intermittent creek to the left and the trail steepness abates slightly. It is not as steep but climbs steadily. There is still another 900 feet of elevation to climb. As you round several ridgelines, the trees break to give great views both north (Spanish Peaks) and south (New Mexico). Several more dikes are encountered and make great places to stop for a snack or lunch. After 3.25 miles from the trailhead, you encounter the intersection with the West Spanish Peak Trail. The peak trail continues up to the right, and the Apishapa Trail is the left fork. The remaining 1.76 miles is good trail with several spectacular overlooks and dikes en route. There is just a bit more climbing on this section, which contains the trail highpoint. Just before the end of the trail at Cordova Pass, there are two beautiful meadows to cross. These open areas provide great views of the peaks and the area you have just climbed. Stop to enjoy your achievement.

This trail works well with a car shuttle drop-off and pick-up, a round trip, or even a bike ride from Cordova Pass to the east trailhead. The entire area is spectacular in the fall.

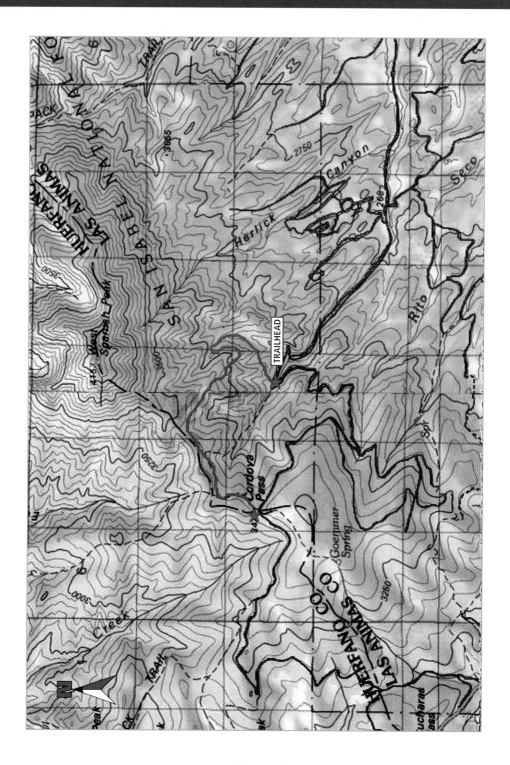

APISHAPA TRAIL

39. Comanche National Grassland— Homestead Trail

BY BRITTANY NIELSON

MAP	USGS, Quad Tub Springs
ELEVATION GAIN	<500 feet
RATING	Easy–moderate
ROUND-TRIP DISTANCE	3.3 miles for Homestead Trail, 4 miles for Arch Rock Trail, 8.7 for Homestead Trail
ROUND-TRIP TIME	2–5 hours
NEAREST LANDMARK	Springfield

COMMENT: Picture Canyon is a treasure chest of history. A surprising find in Southeast Colorado, this hike is farther from the Front Range than other hikes in this book. Although it is beyond the parameters discussed in the introduction, this hike is well worth including. After hours of driving across the flat

Artwork on the rocks.   PHOTO BY BRITTANY NIELSON

Rock Formations in Picture Canyon.

plains of Colorado, the canyon opens up, revealing whimsical rock formations, a nice riparian zone, and an option for multiple loop hikes. Historic features of this canyon include pictographs, petroglyphs, homestead ruins, and dinosaur tracks. (The dinosaur tracks are not marked or identified. Do not expect to actually find the dinosaur tracks here.)

The trails in Picture Canyon are well marked; however, the markings are not always easy to understand. The US Forest Service is aware and has plans to correct this situation. The trip description below is of the Hiker Bypass Trail. The Arch Rock Trail and Homestead Trail loop off the Bypass Trail.

Maps and information regarding this area are sparse. A trail map can be picked up in Springfield at the ranger station, but the map lacks any helpful detail. Other options include tracking down a copy of the US Geological Survey quad map or printing from mapping software.

GETTING THERE: Exit Interstate 25 at exit 15 in Trinidad. Head east on Colorado 160 and follow the signs to remain on 160 for 97 miles. Follow the signs to Picture Canyon, proceeding straight onto a dirt road at the sharp left turn. Take the first right onto County Road 10.

Follow this well-maintained dirt road 10 miles to County Road M. Follow the signs for Picture Canyon and turn left. Drive 8 miles to County Road 18 and turn right. After another 7 miles turn right at the sign for Picture Canyon and drive two miles to the picnic area.

THE ROUTE: Sign the trail register and proceed through the gate. Merge onto the old double track toward the canyon to the left. Less than half a mile into the canyon, take a detour to the left to see petroglyphs.

Proceed back to the trail and head left, continuing deeper into the canyon. Less than 0.1 miles after returning to the trail, turn left again and proceed through a gate. Arrive at a junction and take a quick detour to the left toward the cliff to another ancient site. Return to the trail and head left. Go through the gate, where the canyon opens up and joins another wide canyon. Head toward the sign to the right and follow arrows across the canyon for the Arch Rock and Homestead Loop.

Upon arriving across the canyon, ruins of an old homestead will be obvious. Directly behind the homestead ruins, notice a gated crack in the cliff. This is Crack Cave and is only open on the fall and spring equinoxes. The cave contains numerous petroglyphs.

From the homestead ruins, walk through what looks to be an old fence line into the canyon to the left. Follow the trail up the hill to a high prairie. Aim for the post high on the hill ahead. Once on top of the hill, posts and cairns continue to mark the trail. Upon arriving at a post or cairn, take the time to locate the next one before proceeding.

Skirt the top of the canyon until arriving at the obviously marked descent back into the canyon through a fun, rocky area. At the giant cairn, continue straight down the small chute and keep following the cairns. Follow the trail through this enjoyable canyon. Once almost out of the canyon, double back at the marker to cross the table.

At the other side of the drainage, turn right, following the sign back to the picnic area.

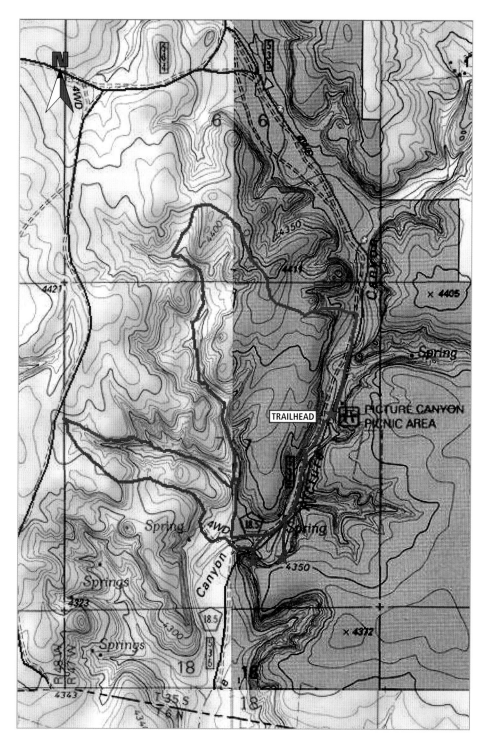

COMANCHE NATIONAL GRASSLAND—HOMESTEAD TRAIL

40. **East Spanish Peak**

BY CAROL NUGENT

MAPS	USGS, Spanish Peaks
ELEVATION GAIN	2,790 feet
RATING	Moderate–difficult
ROUND-TRIP DISTANCE	8.7 miles
ROUND-TRIP TIME	4–6 hours
NEAREST LANDMARK	La Veta

COMMENT: The East Spanish Peak, the smaller and most eastern outlier of the Sangre de Cristo Range, is located in the Spanish Peaks Wilderness of the San Isabel National Forest. In early August the trail begins with lush greenery that

Along the trail to East Spanish Peak.   PHOTO BY GREG LONG

Looking across to West Spanish Peak.   PHOTO BY GREG LONG

abruptly gives way to rocky talus and spectacular views of an ever-widening horizon. The top of the peak provides a special treat in the form of swarming ladybugs.

The trail to the saddle between East Spanish Peak and West Spanish Peak is obvious and well traveled. The hiker's trail from the saddle to treeline requires you to pay a little more attention. Once you reach treeline, you will not find a trail, but your route is the obvious ridgeline.

GETTING THERE: From Walsenburg, travel east on US 160 to Highway 12. Turn south on Highway 12 and travel through La Veta. On the south side of the town, turn east on Cucharas Street, then south on Birch Street, which is also County Road 360. Stay on County Road 360 for approximately 6.5 to 7 miles until you reach the national forest boundary. Within a few hundred yards there is a small road and a gate through the fence on the south side of the road. A small sign on the fence reads *Wahatoya Trail*. This is the road to the trailhead. If you find yourself among cabins, you have missed the road to the trailhead.

To get from County Road 360 to the trailhead, a four-wheel-drive vehicle is recommended. From the gate to the trailhead is approximately 2 miles. If you do not have a vehicle qualified to make the trip to the trailhead, you can park along the road and hike up to the trailhead. The mileage and time provided for the hike are based on parking at the trailhead.

THE ROUTE: From the trailhead, travel east on the gently climbing and contouring trail for approximately 2.25 miles to the saddle between East Spanish Peak and West Spanish Peak. At the saddle you will find a signpost with no sign. At the post, turn left and locate the much fainter hiker's trail. Follow the hiker's trail east. After another 0.5 miles the trail begins to climb rather steeply. If you pause for a break, do not let go of any possession lest it roll back down the hill.

The acute angle subsides after a half mile; continue up the tree-covered ridgeline. The hiker's trail sometimes fades, and there are sometimes several social trails, but it essentially follows the ridge until it reaches treeline.

Treeline is an abrupt transition from forest to talus slope. Take your time on the looser talus. As you climb, the rocks become larger, including a few oddly vertical pillars. The climb up this section of the ridgeline includes a nice high-elevation walk across a not-too-exposed ridge as you make your way to the summit block. It is here that, if the season is right, you begin to notice the ladybugs. As you approach the summit, you will see ladybugs crawling out from under rocks, nestled in crevices, and generally milling about in large quantities. But beware: they bite.

After another short, steep section, you reach the summit (12,683 feet). To the west, enjoy the views of the Sangre de Cristo Range and the West Spanish Peak. Then turn east and admire the far horizon that is uninterrupted by mountains until the Ozarks. After enjoying the views, retrace your steps back down the mountain to your car.

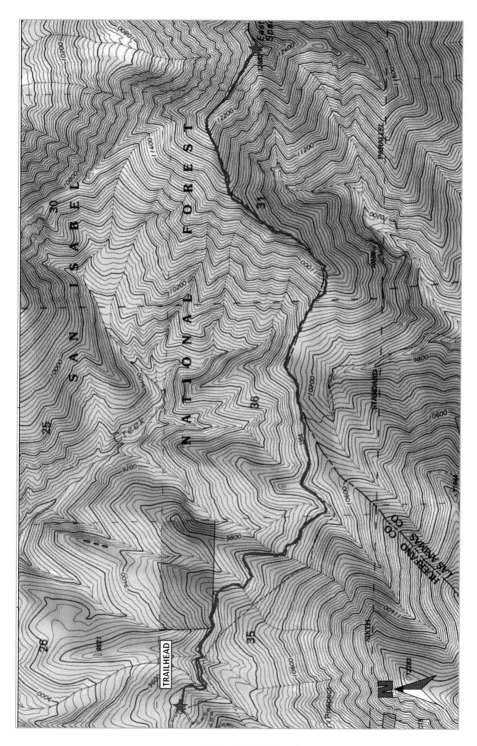

EAST SPANISH PEAK

41. Lathrop State Park— Cuerno Verde Trail

BY BILL HOUGHTON

MAP	Lathrop State Park Handout
ELEVATION GAIN	87 feet
RATING	Easy
ROUND-TRIP DISTANCE	2.9 miles
ROUND-TRIP TIME	1–2 hours
NEAREST LANDMARK	Walsenburg

COMMENT: Cuerno Verde ("Green Horn") is a paved (asphalt) trail around Martin Lake. This lake is one of two larger lakes in Lathrop State Park. Martin Lake is administered by the state parks system, while Horseshoe Lake is managed by the Colorado Division of Wildlife. Martin Lake has all the comforts of home with both an electrified campground and a non-electrified camping area as well as boat docks, picnic areas, a swimming area, and numerous restrooms. Cuerno Verde is a great trail for exercise and can be hiked, biked, skated, or cross-country skied (assuming good snow conditions). It is a family-friendly surface on which young bikers can practice their skills.

GETTING THERE: From Interstate 25, take exit 52 toward Walsenburg. Drive west from Walsenburg 4 miles on Colorado 160 to a prominent sign marking the park entrance. The Cuerno Verde Trail starts from the parking lot at the visitor center.

THE ROUTE: This trail description assumes that you have decided to move counter-clockwise (right at the trail split), but because it is a loop, you can hike either direction. The trail crosses the lake overflow and, later on, follows the shoulder of the road for a few feet but generally is a separate trail that gives quick access to the lake and great views of the lake and the backdrop of the Spanish Peaks. Only 0.25 miles from the parking lot, you get the first open view of the lake from the overflow. Avoid crossing this area while water is flowing here. This is a "no wake" area of the lake so the cattails and ducks may remain undisturbed. After a mile from the parking lot, and at close proximity to the road, a spur from the road leads to the trailhead for the Hogback Trail (description follows). Rounding

Picnic area along the lake.   PHOTO BY BILL HOUGHTON

the north end of the lake and back on a dedicated trail, the picnic areas appear both near and above the lake. This shaded section of trail is welcome in the heat of summer. Soon after the picnic tables end, the trail crosses an intake bridge and approaches the swimming area. Just after the swimming area are the boat dock and a shaded, grassy area from which to observe boating activities and water skiing. Finally, the trail passes a group picnic area and climbs gently back to the visitor center.

SIDEBAR: LATHROP STATE PARK

It's time to celebrate! The Colorado State Parks System has been in existence for a half century. Did anyone mention that we were late starters? The first park in the system was Lathrop State Park. Although originally a series of natural lakes, the current reservoirs were created to fulfill the need for a water storage facility for Walsenburg. Turning off Interstate 25 after miles of bleak, barren eastern plains, one does not expect to be surprised so quickly with large areas of water and the transition zone to forested lands. In another sense, Lathrop State Park includes the spectrum from urban to wild lands. Boasting the only golf course in a Colorado state park, located on its eastern edge, and bear, deer, rattlesnakes, and the rare "tiger muskie" living on the western edge, Lathrop State Park exemplifies this transition.

Because the parks system manages Martin Lake, most of the recreation is located in and around this lake. There are no trails, or plans for them, in or around Horseshoe Lake, but it is worth the time to drive around it. Because Lathrop State Park exists in a transition zone, the most favorable times to visit are in the spring and fall.

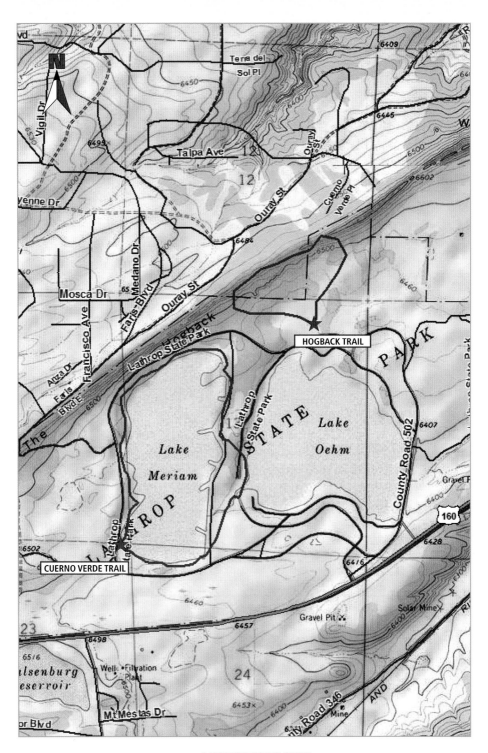

LATHROP STATE PARK

42. Lathrop State Park— Hogback Trail

BY BILL HOUGHTON

MAP	Lathrop State Park Handout
ELEVATION GAIN	209 feet
RATING	Easy
ROUND-TRIP DISTANCE	1.6 miles
ROUND-TRIP TIME	1–2 hours
NEAREST LANDMARK	Walsenburg

COMMENT: The Hogback Trail is more varied and more interesting than the Cuerno Verde Trail. It also gives you a great view over the entire area. A specific guide for this nature trail can be obtained at the visitor center. Initially, the trail climbs gently through piñon, juniper, and sandstone areas before coming to

Enjoying views of the Spanish Peaks from the hogback.   PHOTO BY BILL HOUGHTON

Bridge on the trail.

the foot of the hogback. Like many other formations in the area of the Spanish Peaks, the hogback is an igneous intrusion (dike) where molten lava has risen through a crack in the earth's crust and cooled. Less weather-resistant rock and soil have eroded from the hogback.

GETTING THERE: Follow the directions to the visitor center parking lot given in the Cuerno Verde Trail description in this book. Taking a counter-clockwise direction (right turn) on the perimeter road, drive 1 mile to the signed, right-turn spur road to the trailhead.

THE ROUTE: Climbing a short series of switchbacks leads quickly to the top of the dike for spectacular views from Fisher's Peak to Greenhorn Mountain. The next 0.5 miles follows the ridgeline atop the hogback. Take this part slowly to ensure stepping carefully, and stop to enjoy the views. A good pair of hiking shoes or boots makes this section more enjoyable and safer. At a slight dip in the dike, the trail crosses a sandstone formation that slopes downward. All along the trail, but particularly in this section, beautiful cactus line the trail and reach out to touch the unsuspecting. Speaking of hazards, this area is also perfect territory for rattlesnakes, so keep at least one eye on the environment of the trail. Looping back to the trailhead gives you an opportunity to view your accomplishment and the entire route of the trail. You also may spot roadrunners at the base of the trail, as this author encountered.

43. Levsa Trail and Reilly Canyon Trail

BY GREG LONG

MAP	USGS, Trinidad West
ELEVATION GAIN	50 feet for Levsa; 300 feet for Reilly
RATING	Easy for Levsa; easy–moderate for Reilly
ROUND-TRIP DISTANCE	1.0 miles for Levsa; 8.0 miles for Reilly
ROUND-TRIP TIME	20–30 minutes for Levsa; 2–4 hours for Reilly
NEAREST LANDMARK	Trinidad

COMMENT: Trinidad Lake State Park is a popular destination for camping and boating yet offers plenty of trails for hikers and mountain bikers. The park features two campgrounds with 73 sites, some of which are open year-round. The park is an excellent base of operations for hikes throughout the Trinidad area as well as within the park itself. Surprisingly, even when the park and its campgrounds are full, it is possible to find solitude by hiking out just a short distance from a trailhead. Trinidad has many summer events, so balance your hiking with some cultural attractions or possibly a blues concert.

GETTING THERE: From Interstate 25, take exit 13B, Colorado 12 West. Follow the signs for Colorado 12 carefully, as it twists and turns through town for 3 miles to Trinidad Lake State Park. Drive into Carpios Ridge Campground and park at the large sign for the trails.

THE ROUTE: The Levsa Trail is a 1-mile loop hike from the campground. It features several benches and interpretive signs along the way, as well as some nice overviews of the lake. This is a pleasant hike for families with small children and anyone who wants a short jaunt away from the bustling campground.

Popular with both hikers and mountain bikers, the Reilly Canyon Trail coincides with the Levsa Trail for 0.4 miles, then veers right, roughly paralleling the lake shore without approaching it. The trail consists mostly of dirt,

The view of Fishers Peak from the trail.

gravel, and broken rock. After about a mile, the trail descends into the canyon proper, featuring rock cliff bands and dry creek beds. The trail meanders through many ups and downs but rarely gains or loses more than 50 to 100 feet at one time. From the high points, take in views of Culebra Peak to the west and Fishers Peak to the southeast. When the views disappear, check out the desert plant life, including small cactus and yucca plants. The trail finishes at the paved road after 4.0 miles. Finish by retracing your steps or arrange a car shuttle.

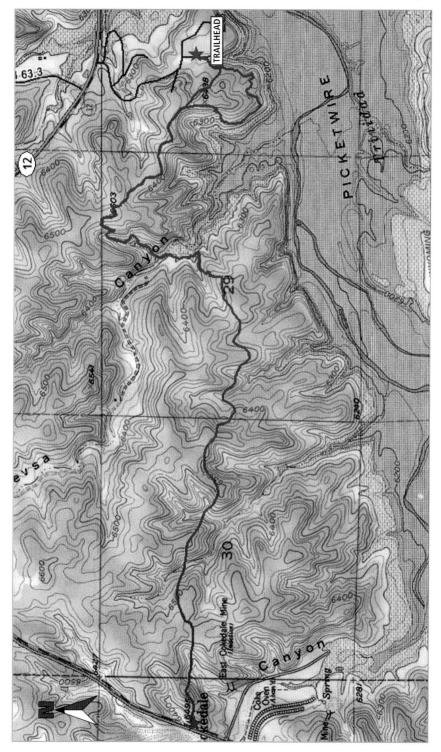

LEVSA TRAIL AND REILLY CANYON TRAIL

44. North Fork Trail

BY BILL HOUGHTON

MAPS	US Forest Service, San Isabel National Forest USGS, Cucharas Pass—1994 Trinchera Peak—1994
ELEVATION GAIN	1,737 feet
RATING	One way—moderate Round trip—moderate–difficult
ROUND-TRIP DISTANCE	8.3 miles
ROUND-TRIP TIME	4–6 hours
NEAREST LANDMARK	North Lake Reservoir

COMMENT: The North Fork Trail follows the north fork of the Purgatoire River. It can be walked in either direction or as an out-and-back from either the north or south trailhead. The most pleasant and accessible trailhead is the south, and this description assumes this option. "Most pleasant" is a relative description, as the road from North Lake Reservoir is rough and rocky but passable by passenger vehicles. The trail starts out as a pleasant walk in the woods at a leisurely climb gradient, although parts of the trail have deteriorated into a rocky, eroded ditch and it feels like walking up a stream bed. Several surprises help to make up for this condition. For example, just up from the trailhead, this author found a yearling bear munching on the late summer raspberries from the middle of the trail and, farther along, passed a great blue heron and a ptarmigan, in turn.

GETTING THERE: The southern trailhead for this hike can be easily accessed from either Walsenburg or Trinidad via the Highway of Legends (Colorado 12). The northern trailhead is 1.1 miles up Forest Service Road 436, requiring a high-clearance four-wheel-drive vehicle from the Blue Lake Campground. (See the description for Trinchera Peak.) The southern access does not require either high clearance or four-wheel drive but is a very rough road. From mile marker 31 on the Highway of Legends, drive north for 4.2 miles to the Purgatoire Campground. Ample trailhead parking can be found inside the campground at the northern end. The signed mileages are incorrect and overstate the distances.

Indian Head Dike, along the North Fork Trail.

THE ROUTE: After starting out on the easy, wooded gradient, the trail continues through mixed aspen and conifers. At about 1.5 miles from the southern trailhead, there appears a mystery lake that is not plotted on any map. This small lake is a good example of eutrophication, as the weeds fill the lake and it will eventually become a meadow. Shortly after this point, at 1.9 miles, a difficult stream crossing may encourage some to make this the turnaround point. This crossing is manageable on horseback but difficult without water shoes or flip-flops. An extensive search upstream by this author revealed several old beaver dams. With Gore-Tex boots, crossing at one of the dams was no problem. After the stream crossing, and up to 3.2 miles from the trailhead, the trail passes through mostly

A tricky creek crossing along the trail.

PHOTO BY BILL HOUGHTON

conifers and is enjoyable. At this point, the trail climbs to the saddle just before the northern trailhead. This is accomplished by going straight up (the horses can handle it) for 700 feet in less than 0.7 miles. The climb is made more difficult by the condition of the trail, which has numerous loose rocks and dirt. There are at least six high-angle climbs broken by a few level or reduced-climb grades that give some hope of eventually reaching the top. And the top does eventually come. The trail traverses a beautiful saddle before joining Trinchera Peak Road. If you've left a car shuttle at the northern (passenger car) parking lot, it is another 1.1 miles down Trinchera Peak Road. On the drive out from the southern trailhead, be sure to notice the red dike on the left side of the road. It naturally resembles an Indian head.

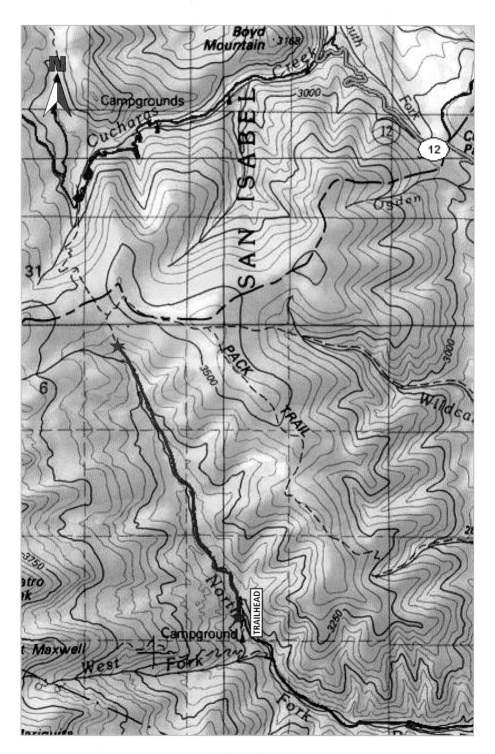

NORTH FORK TRAIL

45. Panadero Loop

BY BILL HOUGHTON

MAPS	US Forest Service, San Isabel National Forest USGS, Cucharas Pass—1994 Trinchera Peak—1994 McCarty Park
ELEVATION GAIN	2,735 feet
RATING	Moderate–difficult
ROUND-TRIP DISTANCE	11 miles
ROUND-TRIP TIME	4–7 hours
NEAREST LANDMARK	Cuchara

COMMENT: The Cuchara Grande Loop consists of five trails that climb into the Sangre de Cristos below Napoleon Peak. There are great views of the West Spanish Peak and the old Cuchara ski area. Hikers encounter 10 stream crossings without bridges, which makes traversing the trail difficult during spring runoff. The first four trails are designed and maintained for all-terrain vehicles (ATVs) so they are wide and moderate to hike.

GETTING THERE: From the intersection of Business Interstate 25 (Main Street) and Colorado 160 (Seventh Street) in Walsenburg, drive west on Colorado 160 for 11.1 miles to Colorado 12. Turn left (south) toward La Veta and continue through the town for 16.6 miles. Watch the turns in La Veta to stay on Colorado 12. At the southern edge of the town of Cuchara, watch for the Spring Creek Trail access and turn right (west). Park and pay ($5 as of this writing).

THE ROUTE: The loop starts on Spring Creek Trail and follows it up to the intersection with Baker and Dodgeton Creek Trails (1.3 miles). Take the right fork (Dodgeton Creek) and proceed for another 2.2 miles. Several stream crossings occur along this segment. At a signed intersection for the Cut Off Trail, turn left and follow this trail for 1.5 miles. At the end of the Cut Off Trail your global positioning system (GPS) should read about 4.9 miles from the trailhead. The Cut Off Trail intersects the Indian Creek Trail. Take the Indian Creek Trail south (left) to the highpoint of the hike at 10,664 feet. Follow the Indian

West Spanish Peak can be seen while hiking the Panadero Loop.   PHOTO BY BILL HOUGHTON

Creek Trail for 1.5 miles to the intersection with the Baker Creek Trail. The Baker Creek Trail is the only segment that is not designed for ATVs and is less maintained. There may be a few downed trees to hop over, and the creek has washed down the trail. Descending the Baker Creek Trail for 2.9 miles takes you back to the Spring Creek Trail along the northern edge of the old ski area. A right turn onto the Spring Creek Trail takes you back to the parking area in 1.3 miles.

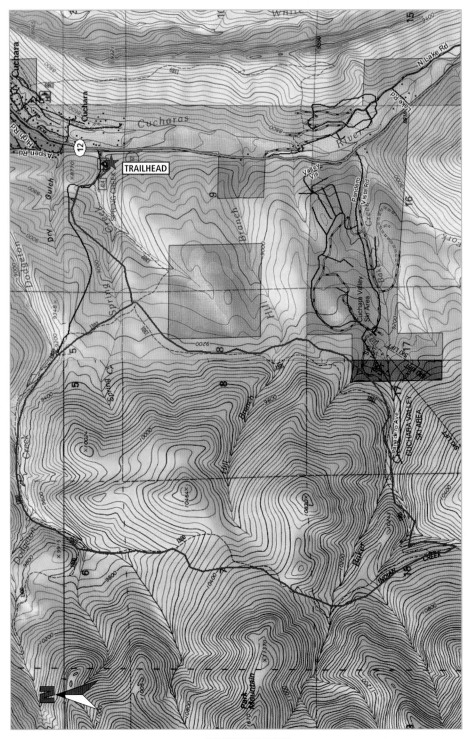

PANADERO LOOP

46. Trinchera Peak

BY BILL HOUGHTON

MAPS	US Forest Service, San Isabel National Forest USGS, Trinchera Peak—1994
ELEVATION GAIN	2,178 feet
RATING	Moderate–difficult
ROUND-TRIP DISTANCE	5.5 miles (Parking at the passenger car area results in a total round trip of 7.7 miles)
ROUND-TRIP TIME	4–6 hours
NEAREST LANDMARK	Cuchara

COMMENT: *Trinchera* is Spanish for "trench." The mountain ranks as a tricentennial—one of the 300 highest peaks in Colorado. The word *trail* is a complete misnomer, as the first part of the hike is on an old mining road and the last part wanders up a ridgeline to the summit without the benefit of a trail. From the top, enjoy views of Culebra Peak, Blanca Peak, and the Spanish Peaks.

The summit peeks out of the clouds.   PHOTO BY BILL HOUGHTON

Sharing the trail with sheep on Trinchera Peak.   PHOTO BY BILL HOUGHTON

GETTING THERE: From the town of Cuchara drive 3.4 miles south on Colorado 12 to the turnoff for Bear Lake and Blue Lakes Campgrounds. Turn right (west) and follow the road for 3.9 miles to the entrance for Blue Lakes Campground. Directly across from this entrance, bear left for 0.1 miles for passenger car parking. High-clearance four-wheel-drive vehicles can drive another 1.1 miles to the North Fork Trailhead. The distances and elevation gained are from this point at 11,339 feet; this is a convenient starting point, as only high-clearance vehicles can technically drive all the way to the crest of the range at 12,800 feet and the road becomes narrower and less safe to drive.

THE ROUTE: Follow the road up to the old mining area. There is not much to look at except for several indentations in the soil where the building used to be. A short spur leads to a shaft entrance. Continue up to the saddle at 12,800 feet. Turn left (south) and discover a series of ledges and a slight indication of previous use. Each time the ledge ends at the crest, move left to the next one, remaining on the east side of the ridge, and proceed up to a flat area at 13,300 feet. Here, the slope angle relents and the remaining 200 feet can be walked on the western slopes. The top is a popular spot, as there are four large cairns. Be observant, as frequently a large herd of bighorn sheep grazes on the southern and western slopes of this mountain. Return by the same trail. In a lightning storm, egress can be made off the south slopes. In that case, carefully note the correct ridge to follow to regain the road down below. Should those grassy slopes beckon, please remember to spread your party to minimize the damage to the tundra.

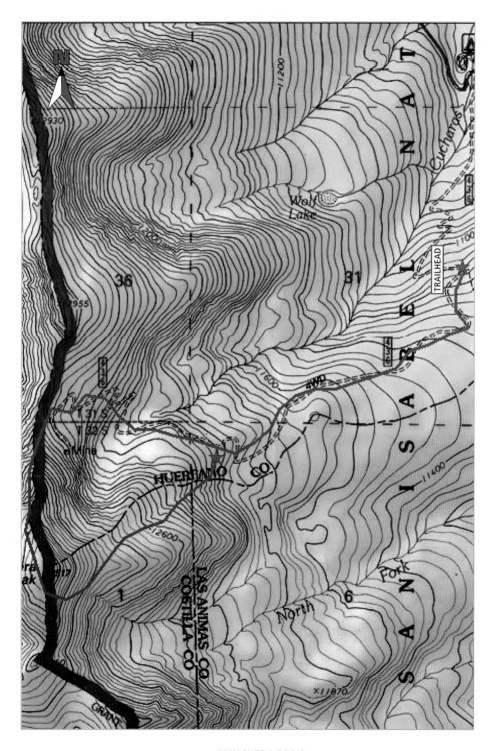

TRINCHERA PEAK

47. Wahatoya Trail

BY BILL HOUGHTON

MAPS	US Forest Service, San Isabel National Forest USGS, Spanish Peaks—1994 Herlick Canyon—1994
ELEVATION GAIN	2,442 feet
RATING	Difficult
ROUND-TRIP DISTANCE	12.6 miles
ROUND-TRIP TIME	5–8 hours
NEAREST LANDMARK	La Veta

COMMENT: This trail passes between the "Breasts of the World," the translation of the Indian word *wahatoya*, which is also the Indian name for the Spanish Peaks. It is a beautiful trail with good tread under foot, mature trees overhead, and spectacular views beyond, but hiking it requires planning to enjoy. It is approached from a dirt road on either end. Much of the southern portion of the trail does not appear on Forest Service or US Geological Survey (USGS) maps yet. The southern trailhead is co-located with the east end of the Apishapa Trail. Approaching from the south, it is 9.2 miles, up 1,200 feet, down 1,900 feet, and back up 1,300 feet to the saddle between East and West Spanish Peaks. From the saddle to the north trailhead is mostly level and spans 2.1 miles. For a shorter hike of 4.2 miles and between one and three hours, approach from the north with a reliable four-wheel-drive vehicle and hike to the saddle and back.

GETTING THERE: This trail requires a high-clearance four-wheel-drive vehicle, a long car shuttle ride, and good map-reading skills, but the views make these preparations worthwhile. The north access is out of the town of La Veta. Driving south on Colorado 12 through the town requires two 90 degree turns. At the second turn, the highway goes west. At this point, leave the highway and go east, following County Road 360. This road also makes several 90-degree turns, before and after it goes past a small lake. The road eventually heads south up the valley. From the turn off Colorado 12 it is 5 miles to the next important turn. This one is partly hidden by a fence; if you reach an area with numerous cabins, you have gone too far. The fence hides a sign on the right side of the

An old Forest Service cabin can be seen on Wahatoya Trail.   PHOTO BY BILL HOUGHTON

road marking the path to the Wahatoya Trailhead. At this point, passenger cars should pull in and park because only high-clearance four-wheel-drive vehicles should attempt the path. The path continues for 2.1 miles to a parking area and the trailhead. The south trailhead is on County Road 46, 23.5 miles west of Aguilar or 11.1 miles east of Cucharas Pass. A car shuttle ride will take about three hours on either end. A four-wheel-drive drop-off and pick-up is a better option if the driver knows the roads and can handle rough, off-road driving.

THE ROUTE: Assuming either an out-and-back or a full trail from the north, the initial trail is reasonably level, climbing 500 feet in 2 miles. It crosses an avalanche chute/stream and two more streams before the saddle. The trail may be level, but the side hills are not, and it is easy to miss a hiking pole plant on the downhill side. Because the trail is forested, the chance of a fall is slight, but the views en route are mostly of the trees.

Dike visible from trail.

At the saddle, a trail to the East Peak turns left while the Wahatoya Trail continues south, straight ahead. The trail then descends 1,300 feet along a branch of the south fork of Trujillo Creek. Another branch joins at an area that has been severely eroded and left a wash that must be crossed, but not at high water. Approaching 9,000 feet, the trail eventually crosses the creek and enters a meadow that contains a sign confirming that you are on the Wahatoya. About 100 feet south another sign directs a right turn (west) up the main valley of the south fork of Trujillo Creek. At this point you are 5.1 miles from the north trailhead and there is an open meadow that invites lunch. Just west of the meadow is the Forest Service cabin indicated on the USGS map of Herlick Canyon. After viewing the locked cabin, return to the trail and turn left to begin a steep climb that switchbacks up several hundred feet and will eventually climb 1,900 feet out of the canyon and along the south slopes of the West Peak. At 9.75 miles from the north trailhead, after spectacular views to the south, the Wahatoya joins the Apishapa Trail and descends 1.5 miles to the trailhead on County Road 46.

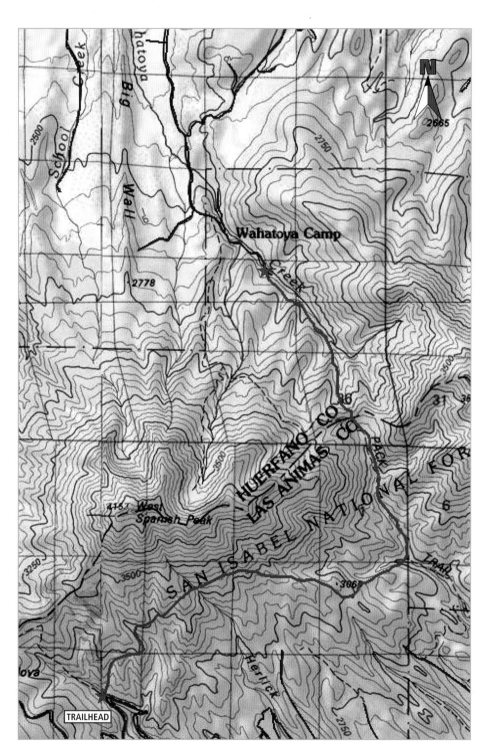

WAHATOYA TRAIL

48. West Spanish Peak Trail

BY BILL HOUGHTON

MAPS	US Forest Service, San Isabel National Forest
	USGS, Spanish Peaks—1994
ELEVATION GAIN	3,010 feet to the summit; 1,300 feet to treeline
RATING	Difficult
ROUND-TRIP DISTANCE	7.5 miles to the summit; 5.8 miles to treeline
ROUND-TRIP TIME	5–8 hours
NEAREST LANDMARK	Cucharas Pass

COMMENT: Walking out on this beautiful trail from the trailhead, you may be wondering why you have not tried it before. Possibly because you thought it was only a climbing trail up to the summit, which it is, but it also gives great views of the Purgatoire and Cuchara river valleys and brings you into close contact with the amazing dikes of the Spanish Peaks. An out-and-back from the trailhead to treeline involves 5.8 miles and 1,300 feet of elevation gained. Spend a half day with the hike, or go full bore and head all the way to the top.

GETTING THERE: From the intersection of Business Interstate 25 (Main Street) and Colorado 160 (Seventh Street) in Walsenburg, drive west on Colorado 160 for 11.1 miles to Colorado 12. Turn left (south) toward La Veta and stay on Colorado 12 through the town for 21.8 miles. Watch the turns in La Veta; be sure to stay on Colorado 12. Drive through the town of Cuchara and up to Cucharas Pass. At the pass, turn left (east) onto Forest Service Road 46. The signs say *to Cordova Pass.* Follow those signs through several potentially confusing turnoffs to the top of that pass in 6.1 miles.

THE ROUTE: Set out from the trailhead and reach treeline after 2.9 miles and 800 feet of elevation gained. From the large cairn at treeline, you are looking almost straight up the southwest ridge—an elevation gain of 1,600 feet in 0.9 miles. It is a rigorous climb. The route to the top is not obvious from the cairn. It follows the southwest ridgeline slightly to the climber's right of the ridge. Except for the first rock field, previous climbers have worn the route down to dirt. Stay close to the ridge and right of several rock bands on the way to the ridgeline just below the summit. From there, it is an easy walk (at 13,500

Navigating a snowfield, with Culebra Peak in the background.   PHOTO BY BILL HOUGHTON

feet) to the summit. Each of three points along the summit ridge appears to be higher when viewed from another. The western point is the summit. Be careful about knocking rocks down on the descent. The full round trip to the peak is 7.5 miles and 3,010 feet of elevation gained, including 500 feet on the return to the parking lot.

SIDEBAR: THE DIKES OF THE SPANISH PEAKS REGION

In countless cars approaching the Spanish Peaks for the first time, the question often comes up, "What is that? It looks like some sort of really long wall."

That is a dike. According to the *American Heritage Dictionary*, a dike is "[a] body of igneous rock that cuts across the structure of adjoining rock, usually as a result of the intrusion of magma. Dikes are often of a different composition from the rock they cut across. They are usually on the order of centimeters to meters across and up to tens of kilometers long." There are three major sets of dikes in the Spanish Peaks region: one around West Spanish Peak, another around Silver Mountain, and a third that runs more or less easterly through the area. These formations make for fascinating viewing up close or from a distance and are most visible from the West Spanish Peak, Wahatoya, and Apishapa Trails in this guide.

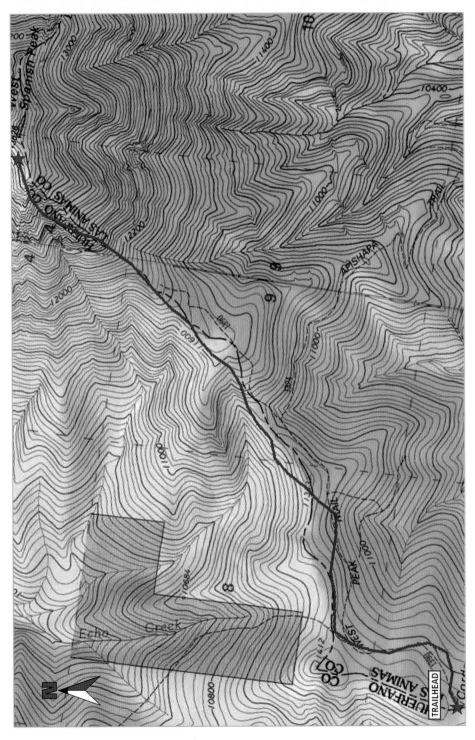

WEST SPANISH PEAK

49. Carpenter Peak

BY SHARON ADAMS

MAPS	Trails Illustrated, Deckers/Rampart Range, Number 135 Free park map at the entrance
ELEVATION GAIN	1,000 feet
RATING	Moderate
ROUND-TRIP DISTANCE	6.4 miles
ROUND-TRIP TIME	3–4 hours
NEAREST LANDMARK	Roxborough Village

COMMENT: Why this hike? Step aside, Garden of the Gods. Roxborough Park has beautiful red rock formations at the beginning of your hike and spectacular views of the Front Range and Denver from the summit. It is open year-round, so bring your snowshoes or cross-country skis in the winter. The lush scrub oak and mountain mahogany provide a beautiful fall hike. If you are looking for a place to take out-of-town guests to experience a taste of Colorado, this is a great choice. It is only a short drive from metropolitan Denver, and the hike stays at a lower altitude.

Carpenter Peak is a family-friendly destination. The Roxborough State Park Visitor Center offers many programs for children and adults. Pick up the publication "Roxborough Rambles" at the entrance gate for a schedule of activities, or visit the center.

GETTING THERE: From South Sante Fe Avenue, head south on Sante Fe, US 85, 4 miles south of Colorado 470, and exit on Titan Parkway. Head west (right); after 3 miles, the road curves to the south (left) and becomes Rampart Range Road. Continue south past Waterton Canyon Road and Roxborough Village. Turn left on Roxborough Park Road and make an immediate right (in about 50 yards) into the Roxborough State Park entrance. Stop at the gate and pay the fee or show your Colorado State Parks Pass. Continue on this road another 2 miles to the visitor center. It is worth the time to walk through it: area experts are available to answer questions, and the center has books, an auditorium for lectures, interpretive displays, and restrooms.

If driving from Wadsworth and Colorado 470, head 5 miles south on Wadsworth from 470 until you come to Waterton Canyon Road. Turn left and head east until the road ends at Rampart Range Road. Turn right and head south on

Kids enjoying the summit of Carpenter Peak. PHOTO BY BOB DAWSON

Rampart Range Road. Follow the instructions above once you are on Rampart Range Road.

THE ROUTE: The well-marked trail is easy to follow. Begin from the visitor center by crossing the park road. The sign reads *Willow Creek Loop, South Rim Loop, Carpenter Peak Trail.* Follow this trail 0.4 miles to a fork and stay to your right. The next sign reads *South Rim Trail, Carpenter Peak Trail.* Go another 0.1 miles to another sign and stay to your right. Look for the sign marked *Carpenter Peak, Colorado Trail.* Cross an open meadow with cottonwood trees and a road. Look for a sign stating *Carpenter Peak, 2.6 miles.* Here begins the gradual uphill switchbacks. Take special care to watch for wildlife—especially at dawn and dusk. At 1.85 miles from the visitor center, you will come to another sign and a fork in the trail. Again, stay right, and follow the signs to Carpenter Peak. The trail levels out and occasional park benches are available.

You will see peaks ahead of you. Carpenter Peak is the right-most peak in the group, with some rocks visible at the top. Continue toward the peaks. You will come to the last sign depicting Carpenter Peak; stay right. A few rocks here require a bit of easy scrambling to the top. After basking in the views, retrace your steps to the visitor center.

Park hours are 7:00 a.m. to 9:00 p.m. in the summer. The visitor center's hours are 9:00 a.m. to 4:00 p.m. weekdays and 9:00 a.m. to 5:00 p.m. weekends in the summer. Visit the visitor center website for non-summer hours and the holiday schedule. No pets or bikes are allowed; day use only.

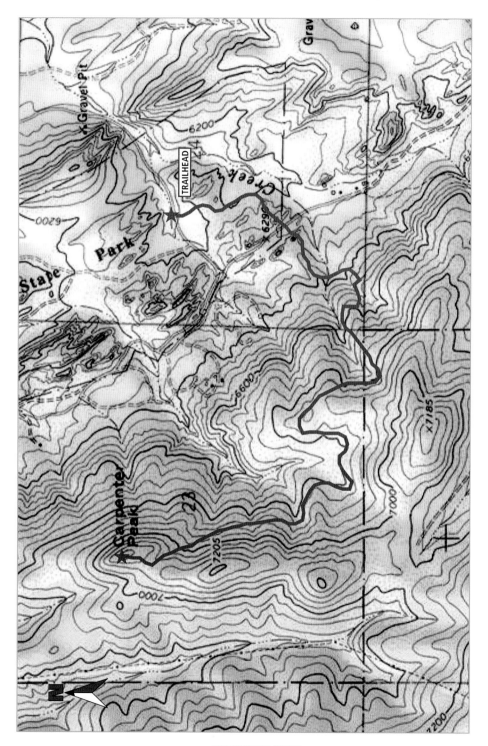

CARPENTER PEAK

50. Castlewood Canyon

BY DWIGHT SUNWALL

MAPS	Obtain maps at the Colorado State Parks website or at park entrance booths
ELEVATION GAIN	1,500 feet
RATING	Easy–moderate
ROUND-TRIP DISTANCE	11.5 miles
ROUND-TRIP TIME	5–6 hours
NEAREST LANDMARK	Franktown

COMMENT: Cherry Creek carves through beautiful Castlewood Canyon as it nears Franktown from its beginning in southeast Douglas County. Castlewood Canyon State Park preserves 2,303 acres of the ecologically unique Black Forest region of Colorado. Trails along the creek wind past the ruins of the Castlewood Dam (circa 1890). On August 3, 1933, the dam broke and caused the second worst flood in Denver's history. Hikers will enjoy spectacular panoramic views of the Front Range and Pikes Peak. The canyon wall harbors hundreds of climbing routes and is a premier top-roping crag.

GETTING THERE: From the north, take Interstate 25 to Founders Parkway, exit 184. Head east, eventually curving south and intersecting Colorado 86 from Castle Rock. Turn left, heading west on US 86. There are two entrances to Castlewood Canyon State Park. The west entrance is accessed from Castlewood Canyon Road off of Colorado 86, 0.5 miles before (west of) Franktown. Look sharp for the road sign and turn right (south), then continue 2.25 miles to the park. The main (or east) entrance is off of US 83. Take US 86 into Franktown. At the traffic light, turn south to US 83 and go 5 miles to the park entrance. From the South, take Interstate 25 to Wilcox Street, exit 181. Turn left onto Wilcox and follow to Fifth Street. Turn right onto Fifth Street; this is Colorado 86. Follow directions above.

THE ROUTE: Castlewood Canyon is divided into three areas: the West Canyon, the Inner Canyon, and the East Preservation Area. Shorter loop hikes can be taken in each area. This description combines all three into one half-day

The Falls Trail in the inner canyon. PHOTO BY DWIGHT SUNWALL

hike. The trails can be accessed from the main east entrance or from the west entrance. This description starts from the west entrance booth.

Park at the Homestead Trailhead and start toward the old concrete building. Take the first right onto the Cherry Creek Trail and follow it 0.6 miles. Pass a parking area with bathrooms and proceed to another nearby lot. Go to the north end of this parking area, cross the road, and take the climbers' trail west, turning left (south) at the wall. Follow the base of the climbing walls 0.3 miles, where the trail returns to the road. Cross the road and take the Fall Spur Trail past the falls along the creek bottom to the dam. South of the dam, cross the creek on a small bridge and hike east to enter the Inner Canyon.

Follow the Inner Canyon Trail until it winds up the canyon rim. Follow the rim east on the nature trail, pass the east entrance, and find the beginning of the East Canyon Preservation Area Trail. The sign marking this trail is about 100 feet south of the sidewalk, on a not-so-obvious dirt trail. The East Canyon Trail is 4 miles out and back, with a loop into the prairie. After returning to the east entrance, follow the sidewalks past the pavilion and gain the Lake Gulch Trail, which drops down to the west end of the inner portion of the canyon. Before the dam, take a right and gain the Rim Trail. The Rim Trail climbs steeply northeast

The East Preservation Trail.   PHOTO BY DWIGHT SUNWALL

from the creek bottom to the rim, and north, a little more than 2 miles, then drops down to the creek again. Cross the creek and return to the Homestead parking area.

The West Canyon loop includes the Climbers' Trail to the dam, the rim route, and the north creek bottom. This loop is 4.5 miles. The Inner Canyon and Lake Gulch loop is 2.5 to 3 miles, depending on how much of the picnic area is hiked. The East Preservation Area loop is 4 miles total, out and back, from the east entrance.

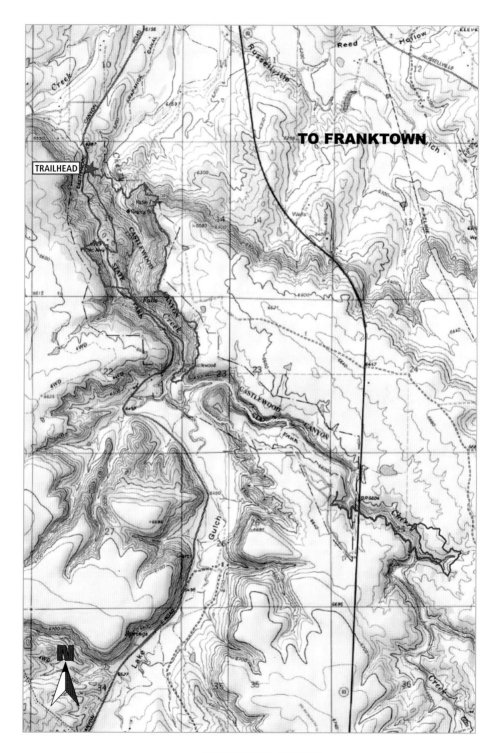

TO FRANKTOWN

TRAILHEAD

CASTLEWOOD CANYON

51. Chautauqua Mountain

BY GREG LONG

MAPS	USGS, Mt. Deception Trails Illustrated, Pikes Peak/ Cañon City, Number 137
ELEVATION GAIN	1,300 feet
RATING	Moderate
ROUND-TRIP DISTANCE	7.5 miles
ROUND-TRIP TIME	3–4 hours
NEAREST LANDMARK	Palmer Lake

COMMENT: Sitting right above the popular Palmer Lake reservoir trails, Chautauqua offers a chance to bag a peak and enjoy some rock scrambling while leaving some of the crowds on the reservoir road behind. The peak is named for the Rocky Mountain Chautauqua Assembly that was active in the town during the late 1800s. The Chautauqua assemblies provided entertainment and inspiration in outdoor settings throughout the United States around the turn of the twentieth century. The Palmer Lake Historical Society has recently begun re-creating these historic gatherings.

The Pike National Forest stretches west to the horizon.　　PHOTO BY GREG LONG

Rock formations visible along the trail.

Upper reservoir.

GETTING THERE: Take Interstate 25 to the Monument/Palmer Lake exit 161. From the northbound exit, turn left onto Colorado 105 and follow it when it turns right after crossing Interstate 25. From the southbound exit, go straight onto Colorado 105. Follow 105 for 3.8 miles and watch for a *Speed Limit 30* sign on the right; turn left onto South Valley Road (the road sign is not visible until after you've made the turn). Drive west on South Valley Road 0.4 miles and turn left on Old Carriage Road. Park at the bottom of the hill.

THE ROUTE: Follow a quarter-mile-long approach trail and join the reservoir service road. Climb this rather steep road for 0.6 miles to reach the first reservoir. Continue on the road to reach the upper reservoir at 1.2 miles and the end of the reservoir at 1.7 miles. Pass a torn-up gate and, at 1.8 miles, turn left and cross over a creek. Turn right and continue on the road uphill. The road takes a 90 degree left turn at 2.4 miles before taking a 90 degree right turn at 2.6 miles. At this right turn, turn left instead up the steep, rutted remnants of a road. The road fades to a faint trail and flattens out at the top of this rise, but this is not the summit. Continue 0.3 miles along the ridge to reach the true summit. The highest point is on top of the rocks; climb to the top.

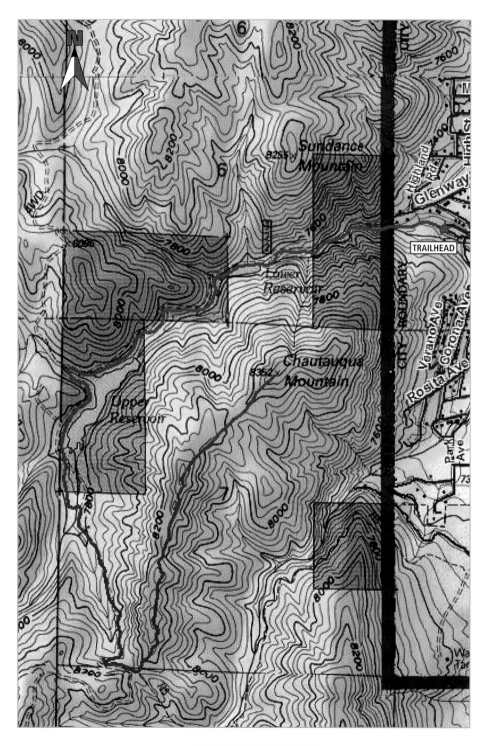

CHAUTAUQUA MOUNTAIN

52. Devils Head

BY GREG LONG

MAP	Trails Illustrated, Deckers/Rampart Range, Number 135
ELEVATION GAIN	850 feet to top of trail, an additional 100 feet to tower
RATING	Easy
ROUND-TRIP DISTANCE	2.8 miles
ROUND-TRIP TIME	2–3 hours
NEAREST LANDMARK	Sedalia

COMMENT: The hike up Devils Head is the best family hike in this book, if not the state of Colorado. It features a wide, well-groomed trail, lots of rocks along the way on which to take a break or scramble around, and a fire tower at the top staffed by a friendly ranger who gives out certificates to hikers who make it to the top, awarding them membership in the Ancient and Honorable Order of the Squirrels. On a recent visit, the author shared the trail with parents pushing

Looking east from the top of Devils Head.   PHOTO BY GREG LONG

Walkway to the fire tower.   PHOTO BY GREG LONG

babies in strollers or carrying them in swaddles, a young man of two-and-a-half years who completed the hike to the tower under his own power, numerous dogs, and even one or two grandparents with canes. A forest service campground at the base of the trail provides the option to spend a full day or weekend on the outing.

GETTING THERE: From Interstate 25, take exit 184, Meadows Parkway. Follow signs to U.S. 85, Sante Fe Drive, and turn right (north) for 5 miles to Colorado 67. Turn left and go 9.5 miles to Rampart Range Road. Turn left and go 9 miles, following the signs to the Devils Head parking area.

THE ROUTE: Follow the well-groomed trail through numerous rock formations and past occasional benches and picnic tables. There is a creek crossing 0.25 miles in; this is the last water for any four-legged friends who might accompany you on the trail. A sign indicates the halfway point, and a short section of cement marks the trail at 0.75 miles. Top out at an open meadow with an old house nearby. Now the fun starts. There are 143 steps up to the fire tower plus 6 more to get into the tower itself. Take a challenge and try to do them without stopping.

The Devils Head Trail is family- and dog-friendly.   PHOTO BY KRISTINA KILCOYNE

From the tower, the Pike National Forest stretches out below, with its namesake mountain visible to the south. Return the way you came.

SIDEBAR: DEVILS HEAD FIRE TOWER

The fire tower at Devils Head is the last manned fire tower in Colorado. Fire lookouts have staffed Devils Head since 1912, when a small table bolted to the rock was all the equipment they had. Soon, a small shelter was added to protect the lookout during storms. In 1919, an enclosed lookout tower was constructed along with a bunkhouse 200 feet below the tower. In 1951, members of the 973rd Engineer Construction Battalion from Fort Carson tore down the original tower and built the present one, along with the infamous stairs to the top. Still going strong at more than 60 years old, the Devils Head fire tower is truly a treasure of the Front Range.

DEVILS HEAD

53. Spruce Mountain

BY GREG LONG

MAP	USGS, Larkspur
ELEVATION GAIN	600 feet
RATING	Easy
ROUND-TRIP DISTANCE	5.5 miles
ROUND-TRIP TIME	2–4 hours
NEAREST LANDMARK	Palmer Lake

COMMENT: The Spruce Mountain Open Space and adjoining Greenland Open Space provide a variety of recreational opportunities in Douglas County, about halfway between Denver and Colorado Springs. Regularly accessed by hikers, bikers, and equestrians in the summer and snowshoers and skiers in the winter, this area has something for everyone.

GETTING THERE: From the north, take Interstate 25 to Larkspur, exit 173. Continue south on Spruce Mountain Road for 6 miles. The trailhead is on the right.

Formation near the trailhead.   PHOTO BY GREG LONG

Rock cliffs near windy point.

From the south, take I-25 to County Line Road, exit 163. Turn left and go 2 miles to Palmer Lake. Cross the railroad tracks and turn right onto Spruce Mountain Road. Go 3.5 miles to the trailhead on the left.

THE ROUTE: Go straight from the trailhead for 0.3 miles along the Eagle Pass Trail. Turn left at the sign and begin to climb. Reach the junction with the Oak Shortcut in another 0.3 miles. This is a steep shortcut back to the trailhead, which is useful should you have bad weather on the way down. Continue climbing on switchbacks to the top of the mesa at 0.8 miles. Begin to notice views south to Mt. Herman and Pikes Peak. Continue along the mesa to the sign for the loop trail at 1.6 miles. The loop is 2.3 miles around and can be hiked in either direction. Going counter-clockwise, pass a service road in 0.7 miles, and reach Windy Point after a mile. Windy Point has great views south to Palmer Lake and Pikes Peak. Continuing on the trail, there are benches and picnic tables just off the trail—good spots for a midway break. Continue around the other side of the loop, then return to the trailhead the way you came.

A nice variation on this hike that provides different scenery is to take the Eagle Pass Trail for its full length, where it connects to the service road at 1.7 miles. Turn left and take the service road to the mesa top and its junction with the loop trail shortly before Windy Point. Return via the loop trail or by retracing your steps.

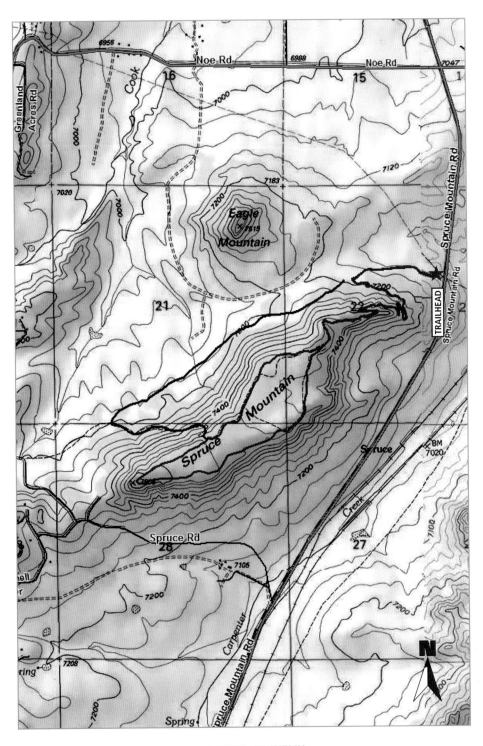

SPRUCE MOUNTAIN

54. Sundance Mountain— Palmer Lake Reservoir Loop

BY GREG LONG

MAP	Trails Illustrated, Pikes Peak/Cañon City, Number 137
ELEVATION GAIN	1,200 feet for Sundance; 1,500 feet for full loop
RATING	Moderate
ROUND-TRIP DISTANCE	3.1 miles for Sundance; 5.0 miles for full loop
ROUND-TRIP TIME	3–4 hours
NEAREST LANDMARK	Palmer Lake

COMMENT: Every year between Thanksgiving and New Year's, commuters on Interstate 25 enjoy seeing a large star lit up on the hills west of the highway. The star is on the east face of Sundance Mountain. Thinking of Sundance only as "that peak with the star on it" belies a strenuous workout and some great views of Pikes Peak. Year-round trailhead access can make this a good snowshoe trip in the winter as well as a hike in the summer.

GETTING THERE: Take Interstate 25 to the Monument/Palmer Lake exit 161. From the northbound exit, turn left onto Colorado 105 and follow it when it turns right after crossing I-25. From the southbound exit, go straight onto Colorado 105. Follow 105 for 3.8 miles and watch for a *Speed Limit 30* sign on the right; turn left onto South Valley Road (the road sign is not visible until after you've made the turn). Drive west on South Valley Road 0.4 miles and turn left on Old Carriage Road. Park at the bottom of the hill.

THE ROUTE: Follow a quarter-mile-long approach trail and join the reservoir service road. Climb this rather steep road for 0.6 miles to reach the first reservoir. Turn right onto an unmarked trail and climb on single track, steeply at times, on the dirt and gravel trail. At 1.4 miles, reach the top of the ridge and turn right. Note this turn should you decide to retrace your steps; it's easily missed on the way down. After a tenth of a mile, an informal trail leads right to the apparent high point, with great views down into town with Ben Lomand cliff looming above the town's namesake lake. The true summit is another 100

Looking toward Cap Rock at Sundance Mountain.   PHOTO BY GREG LONG

yards south along the ridge. Stand on the rocks just below the summit for good views of Pikes Peak.

Retrace your steps to return to the trailhead, or take a scenic loop along some of the lesser-traveled side trails to the upper reservoir. To make the loop, return to the main trail and begin to retrace your steps; pass the trail you came up and continue another 0.2 miles. Bear left and drop steeply off the ridge. Reach a trail junction at the bottom of the hill and turn left. In another quarter mile, bear right at the junction with the Ice Cave Creek trail. Pass some campsites and cross a creek before climbing to a small ridge. Continue straight at the top of the ridge and begin descending toward the upper reservoir. Stay left at a fork and then turn left on the reservoir road. Walk along the shore of the reservoir, a great

View of Ben Lomand above Palmer Lake.   PHOTO BY GREG LONG

spot for a picnic lunch or to drop a line, before descending 1.2 miles on the road back to the parking lot.

SIDEBAR: RAMPART EAST ROADLESS AREA

From Sundance Mountain north toward Denver is the proposed Rampart East Roadless Area. It includes 30,000 acres that would provide an oasis of solitude and quiet-use recreation in the heart of the Front Range. Featuring unique rock formations, mountain and prairie views, and a variety of flowers and wildlife, the area is a rare gem in the increasingly crowded Front Range. Several rare or imperiled species are found in Rampart East; these include birds (peregrine falcons and the Mexican Spotted Owl), insects, mammals, and several species of plants. The Colorado Mountain Club is working to protect this unique area from future development and off-road motorized use. For information on the area, check out www.cmc.org/rera.

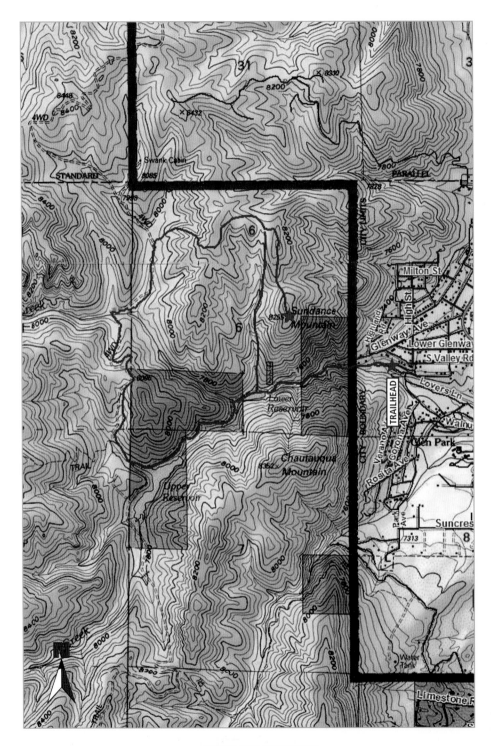

SUNDANCE MOUNTAIN

Checklist of Hikes

ROUTE	PAGE	HIKING PARTNER	DATE
☐ Aiken Canyon	18		
☐ Almagre Mountain	21		
☐ Apishapa Trail	141		
☐ Arkansas Point	91		
☐ Barr Trail to Pikes Peak	24		
☐ Bison Peak	29		
☐ Bushnell Lakes	95		
☐ California Peak	98		
☐ Carpenter Peak	177		
☐ Castlewood Canyon	180		
☐ Chautauqua Mountain	184		
☐ Cheyenne Mountain State Park	32		
☐ Comanche National Grassland—Homestead Trail	144		
☐ Comanche-Venable Loop	101		
☐ Curley Peak	105		
☐ Devils Head	188		
☐ Dome Rock Loop	36		
☐ Dry Creek Trail	108		
☐ Eagle Peak	40		
☐ East Spanish Peak	148		
☐ Florissant Fossil Beds National Monument	44		
☐ Fox Run Regional Park— North Loop	48		
☐ Garden of the Gods—Central Garden/Rockledge Ranch Loop	51		
☐ Goodwin Lakes Trail	111		
☐ Grayback Peak	55		
☐ Greenhorn Mountain	114		
☐ Heizer Trail	58		
☐ Horn Peak	117		

ROUTE	PAGE	HIKING PARTNER	DATE
☐ Lathrop State Park—Cuerno Verde Trail	152		
☐ Lathrop State Park—Hogback Trail	155		
☐ Levsa Trail and Reilly Canyon Trail	157		
☐ Lily Lake	120		
☐ Monument Rock Loop	61		
☐ Mount Esther	64		
☐ Mount Lindsey	123		
☐ Mueller State Park—Homestead, Beaver Ponds, Rock Pond Loop	67		
☐ Newlin Creek Trail	126		
☐ North Fork Trail	160		
☐ Paint Mines Interpretive Park	71		
☐ Panadero Loop	164		
☐ Pipeline Trail to Emerald Valley	74		
☐ Pueblo Riverwalk	129		
☐ Rainbow Trail	132		
☐ St. Charles Peak	135		
☐ Stanley Canyon Trail	77		
☐ Spruce Mountain	192		
☐ Sundance Mountain—Palmer Lake Reservoir Loop	195		
☐ Tower Trail—Pueblo Mountain Park	138		
☐ Trinchera Peak	167		
☐ Ute Valley Park	81		
☐ Wahatoya Trail	170		
☐ Waldo Canyon	84		
☐ West Spanish Peak Trail	174		
☐ Williams Canyon	87		